From Prisoner of Man to
Victory & Freedom in Christ

"WHY ME"

D0877552

BOOKER T. BLEDSOE

Why Me?: From Prisoner of Man to Freedom in Christ
© 2016 by Booker T. Bledsoe

ISBN: 978-0-692-50313-3

AUTHOR BIO

After graduating with a B/S degree in Business Administration from Drexel University, Booker Bledsoe began a ten-year career as a criminal investigator with the Internal Revenue Service, moving into management before being dismissed as a result of a drug addiction. He soon became a convicted felon and served nearly three years in the state penitentiary. Upon his release, Booker worked in the substance abuse treatment field before retiring after 25 years. His vocation now is to be a mentor to men who do not yet know the Lord. Booker currently resides with his wife, Debbie, and their two youngest sons in Southern California.

Contact Booker T. Bledsoe at:
bblessed247@verizon.net
www.WhyMeTheBook.net

I, therefore, the prisoner of the Lord, beseech you that ye walk worthy of the vocation wherewith ye are called.

EPHESIANS 4:1

DEDICATION

I would like to dedicate this book to my wife of 28 years, Debra, without her positive energy and encouragement this project would still be on the shelf. To each of my children; Bridgette, Rasheed, Kito (deceased), Octavious, Josiah and Joel. To my sister-in-law, Erica Brown, who has become like a second daughter to me. A fond farewell to my mom, Marie, without whom none of my successes would have been possible.

CONTENTS

INTRODUCTION

EVERYONE HAS *WHY me* moments. The thought may come and go, or it can be the beginning of a pity party that lasts a lifetime.

It's been twenty-five years since the astonishing chain of *why me* events changed the course of my life forever. It seems like only yesterday. The lessons are still relevant. Someone needs to hear. Someone will listen. A life will be saved. A mother will be comforted. A father will remain hopeful. I pray this project will bless all who read it.

Everyone also has *aha* moments—that instant when it dawns that something extremely significant has just happened. Your eyes are opened to a new and exciting idea. That moment freezes time and allows your thoughts and feelings to blossom. The aha is a special revelation that may come only once in a lifetime.

Eeyore, the donkey character in Winnie the Pooh stories, has plenty of *why me* moments. Unfortunately, his are all negative. By sharing my *why me* story, I hope to open your mind to the *aha* moments that show how even a *why me* can be a blessing. If you consider it, I think you'll find that there have been plenty of positive *why me's* that have come about in your life. Whether or not they turn into blessings depends a lot on you as well.

It is my desire that my story will help you to see your story in a new way that moves you into a life of blessing and faith. Then your story will in turn bless many more. So at key moments, I will pause to help you along in your own story. Call me your Big Bro Booker as we take this journey together.

> And we know that all things work together for good to them that love God, to them who are the called according to His purpose. —Romans 8:28

We are all called into a higher purpose. It's my honor to help you discover and live in it.

PART ONE

THE OLD LIFE

THAT YE PUT OFF, CONCERNING THE FORMER CONVERSATION THE OLD MAN
WHICH IS CORRUPT ACCORDING TO THE DECEITFUL LUSTS.
—EPHESIANS 4:22

MEETING JESUS ON THE RUN

ON A WARM September evening in 1985, we had just finished eating the salmon croquettes Uncle Buddy had prepared for dinner. My three kids were doing whatever kids do between dinner and bedtime. My mom and stepfather were in their room.

My uncle had taken his usual position in a chair on the front stoop, waving at nearly every car that went by. The smoke from the Pall Mall cigarettes he loved encircled his wavy hair.

I pretended to watch Monday Night Football. The Rams were playing the Eagles, but my mind was far from the game.

Drugs had been part of my life for quite some time. I had smoked marijuana since high school. The habit continued through college and somehow went undetected during ten years of employment as a special agent with the Internal Revenue Service's Criminal Investigation Division. During my employment, I had even served on presidential protection details while under the influence.

I had once argued with my mom that God wouldn't have put pot here if He didn't want us to enjoy it. How wrong I was! Marijuana was my gateway drug, the mind-altering substance that made most other things okay. Reefer led to cocaine, which led to crack—what we called at the time freebase.

I told my mom I was headed to my real estate broker class. A lie I had made up a few weeks earlier to cover my absence during robbery efforts. Besides, I had to have some semblance of a productive future. I had lost my job with the IRS in March of 1984.

I had staked out a liquor store close to the freeway—that made for a quick getaway in either direction. I guess this was my modus operandi—almost routine. Despite being a former federal law enforcement officer, the son of a Cleveland police detective, I had turned to the unspeakable. Robbery, and robbery of a liquor store at that. How often I had joked with my IRS buddies, saying how crazy liquor store robbers were. I'd vowed if I ever decided to rob something it would be a bank. Banks were safer and the money was better.

After saying my "see you laters" to my uncle and the kids, I jumped into my mom's car and headed to Ontario, California, a short trip down the freeway from Pomona.

When I arrived at my destination, I did the usual: I asked God to watch over me. I actually asked God to protect me as I blatantly broke the eighth of His Ten Commandments. I parked and walked slowly towards the liquor store. I wore a jacket to cover my son's pellet gun, which I had stuffed into the waistband of my pants. Wearing a jacket on a hot late-summer evening was as much a giveaway as the gun.

I walked up to the cash register and asked for a pint of rum. The only person I saw was the clerk. She got the bottle and set it on the counter.

Now the hard part—closing the deal. At a previous robbery, I had actually told the clerk I was sorry and asked him to forgive me. Why? I guess that was just the type of person I was, polite but slightly insane. I pulled the "gun" and demanded all the money in the register.

The clerk screamed.

We were not alone.

A man stood up from behind the counter to the left of the register. He was between me and the door, and he had a gun.

He fired.

Instinctively, I lifted my left hand to block the bullet. The first shot struck my hand. He got off five more rounds, each of them missing. I was paralyzed with fear until the shooting stopped.

I ran out the door.

A commotion rose at the Laundromat next door as they tried to figure out whether they had heard gunshots.

I sprinted to the car. My feet slid as I tried to stop and I went past the door, but grabbed the handle. The freeway was only a traffic light away. Although there was no oncoming traffic, I actually stopped at the light. This short span of robberies hadn't entirely erased my years as a law-abiding citizen.

But then I ran the light and pulled onto the ramp. I rolled down my window and tossed the pellet gun out, across the top of the car and into some bushes.

WHY ME?

WHY DID I SURVIVE SIX CLOSE-RANGE GUN SHOTS WITH ONLY A HAND WOUND? WAS IT LUCK, OR DID GOD REALLY HEAR MY PRAYERS TO PROTECT ME DURING THE ROBBERY? WHAT WAS HE THINKING?

My hand was a mess, bleeding profusely. The hole on the inside of my hand was fairly small, but the outside was blown totally open. The hollow-point bullet had gone all the way through. My hand burned like fire.

I shouted at the top of my lungs, "Thank you Jesus, thank you Jesus," as I pulled onto the freeway and headed to the hospital in Pomona. I kept thanking Him until I got there.

Many times during my cocaine addiction I had realized things were way out of control. I had done things I never thought I would stoop to. Leaving my kids at home unsupervised when I figured they were asleep. Putting up with the antics of their mother, who stayed away for days at a time in her own addiction. She no longer even tried to hide her relationships with drugs and other men. I had asked God to get me out of the mess I was in because I didn't know how.

As I parked the car and walked into the emergency room, I knew that my life was about to take a dramatic turn. For better or worse, things were on the verge of changing. I believed that God had stepped in. When God takes control, he's always on time.

It was time.

When I entered the hospital, I told the attendant someone had tried to rob me and shot me in the process. I was immediately taken back, placed in a cubicle, and given a shot to relieve the pain.

As I lay there under the influence of the medication, I noticed a hospital security guard standing watch. Within minutes, a Pomona Police Department officer walked in and spoke with him. They came over to me, and it didn't take much for me to admit my crime.

WHY YOU?

HAVE YOU EVER ASKED GOD TO PROTECT YOU WHILE YOU BROKE HIS RULES? DID YOU GET HURT ANYWAY? WHAT HAPPENED?

A short time later, officers from the Ontario Police Department arrived with the same questions. They asked about the gun, and I told them where I had tossed it. I insisted it wasn't a real gun.

They mentioned that they had found some bullets in a book bag in the car.

I said they were leftovers from my days in law enforcement. I gave the same answers concerning the crime as I had given to the Pomona cops and even began to feel some sort of camaraderie with these guys. I was delirious, I guess, as I spoke of my years of service with the federal government and the arrests I had made.

The two departments haggled over who had jurisdiction. Pomona wanted to take me to LA County Jail and Ontario wanted to take me to the San Bernardino County Jail. I lived in Pomona and the arrest was made in Pomona, in Los Angeles County, but the crime was committed in Ontario, in San Bernardino County.

The pain returned and I quickly bled through the gauze and bandage they had placed over my wound. I asked for pain medication, but the police blocked my request. Perhaps they wanted me to be clearheaded and able to give straightforward answers. Or maybe they didn't want me to feel too comfortable. Could they have wanted me to be in a position of need, willing to say anything to get past the questions and get my medical needs met?

Finally Pomona agreed to let Ontario take me. Although I was already in an acute care hospital, they had determined I was stabilized and needed to be transferred to a county hospital that included a jail ward. There I could be detained as long as necessary.

I was wheeled out to an ambulance. One of the policeman asked the ambulance driver to stop at the crime scene so I could be identified.

Thankfully the driver refused, stating his job was to get me to a hospital.

WHAT ABOUT YOU?

God's wisdom says that the person who "...diligently seeketh good procureth favour: but he that seeketh mischief, it shall come unto him" (Proverbs 11:27)

Have you, like me, prayed to God for help while doing things that break God's laws and the laws of the state?

What favor has come from that?

What trouble has come from that?

If you're only finding trouble and not favor, it's time to sincerely ask God to intervene in your life. Right now is the perfect time to ask Him. You can say,

"Dear God, I am so sorry for the evil things I have done. I want to change. I want to do good because I love you. Please help me to do that, Lord. Please help me."

Now, believe that God will answer your prayer in a just, merciful and loving way, as any good father would do.

IT WASN'T ALWAYS THIS WAY

MY MOM WAS the one person I never wanted to disappoint. She raised me by herself. When my life began, hers stopped. She put every effort into ensuring I made it out of the projects of Pittsburgh. She made sure I spent time with my grandmother in church. My grandfather and uncles were welcomed in our home and shared their work ethic. My mother added to this recipe her hard work and honesty.

It worked for a while.

I not only graduated from high school, in 1974 I earned my degree in business administration from Drexel University and obtained a prestigious job with the government.

I began working with the IRS in 1971 as a student co-op. Upon graduation, I went straight to work for the government as a special agent in the Intelligence Division.

I did well in my mandatory training courses and started a promising career. Although marijuana was a big part of my life, cocaine was yet to raise its ugly head. In 1977 I was transferred to our Los Angeles office, a much bigger and more law-enforcement-oriented place than the Pittsburgh office. Due to its size, promotion came much faster.

There was another reason for moving my family. My wife was unfaithful, and for some reason I thought changing location would change her. My children were my jewels, and I feared losing them if I left her. My dad had left my mom when I was a baby, and I had made a self-commitment to stay with my kids through thick and thin.

In Los Angeles, I moved up the ranks quickly, and within six years I was a group manager. A peer in another state told me there were only five other blacks in the country who had reached the same level as me. I was thirty-two years old.

The shaky home life I had brought with me from Pittsburgh only deteriorated. There were temptations aplenty in LA, and my wife took advantage of my kindness and my willingness to forgive in order to hold the family together.

But the ways of many of my friends and associates eventually caught up to me. Most of them had used drugs. Many were heroin addicts. A few had criminal backgrounds. Somehow, in spite of my successes, I never felt a need to cut ties with these guys. We had grown up together and shared so many life stories.

My only crimes had been breaking into a dorm room at school and driving the escape car in a purse-snatching that brought five of us a total of five dollars—enough for a nickel bag of weed.

Then, of course, there was the actual drug use, which until 1982 was primarily marijuana, with a line of cocaine every now and then. My wife arrived home one evening that spring after a weekend missing in action. She brought me a gift. Crack cocaine.

"Downhill" came quicker than expected.

I welcomed the drug with a sense of unity. In my warped way of thinking, I believed it would bring us closer together.

It didn't.

I was soon in deep financial trouble.

While working undercover with the IRS, I had foolishly bragged to my wife about an assignment that came with a $10,000 account under the name of Jeffrey Stevens (the names of my two half-brothers). I even showed her the checkbook.

Somewhere along the line, she removed some checks and made them out to herself. I never knew it until the time came for me to write a check to the principal under investigation, and the check bounced all the way from London back to Los Angeles.

The assignment was a joint investigation with the FBI, and they were the first to find out. I was quickly contacted by the IRS Internal Security Department.

WHY ME?

WHY DID MY WIFE CHEAT ON ME? WHY DID SHE STEAL FROM ME? WHY DID SHE LEAVE ME? WHY DID SHE GIVE ME DRUGS TO GET ADDICTED TO? BECAUSE "…EVIL COMMUNICATIONS CORRUPT GOOD MANNERS." (1 CORINTHIANS 15:33)

YOU MIGHT ASK, "DIDN'T JESUS HANG OUT WITH EVIL PEOPLE? DIDN'T JESUS HAVE GOOD HABITS?"

YES HE DID, BUT HE NEVER ALLOWED EVIL BEHAVIOR TO CORRUPT GOD'S PLAN FOR HIS OWN LIFE. HE TRIED TO DO GOOD AND SAVE THEIR SOULS—NOT DO EVIL AND LIE, STEAL, OR CHEAT OTHERS, LIKE THOSE EVIL PEOPLE DID.

I explained that my wife had a drug problem, and admitted the money was my responsibility. I never mentioned my own cocaine use, which was in its beginning stages. Immediately I was suspended without pay.

My supervisor, a branch chief, was tearful as he asked me to turn in my badge and weapon.

I caught a bus home and went on a cocaine binge.

I soon pleaded guilty to about thirteen counts of theft of government property—each check was a count. The government took into account my record of employment, which was exemplary, and the fact that I cooperated throughout the investigation. They charged me with misdemeanors, placing me on probation.

The job that had so much to offer was gone.

Then I lost my home.

Once my wife found out there was no other benefit in having me, she left, too.

I still remember my first hit from the pipe, the sensation that no one could overcome the desire for another hit and another and another. There was something about that first hit of the day. It was as close to an orgasm as one could get without having sex—perhaps better.

For the next several years I chased that first-hit feeling through alleys, crack houses, shabby hourly motel rooms, and all sorts of god-forsaken places where danger real or imagined lurked at every turn. Over time the paranoia escalated.

These were dead-end places, where the smell of too many all-nighters hung over lifeless souls who continued to put the pipe to their lips, while those around stared with thirsty eyes as the smoke made its way from pipe to mouth. The sizzle and the medicinal smell brought anticipation, but no speech.

That's what I left behind that fall evening in September 1985.

WHY YOU?

Think of all the wrong, illegal, evil things your friends or relatives do. Which of these same things do you do?

These people help to bring big troubles into your life. Maybe trouble has already come. If so, what has happened?

If not, maybe trouble will come next week. Saying good-bye to corrupt friends is like saying good-bye to cocaine or alcohol or any addicted substance—it's difficult, but it will likely save your life.

"Aha!"— You might say, "I will be friends with these people and try to save their souls, like Jesus did. I will do good while they do bad."

That's a nice promise, but it will never work until you have been invaded by God and personally encountered God's love, justice, and mercy on your life. This will give you the courage and power to not be corrupted by evil, as Jesus did.

Yes, you can really encounter God. Until then, you will be too weak to say no to any offer by your friends to do bad.

Ask God to help you leave all bad influences.

ALL I REALLY WANTED WAS A BABY RUTH

WHEN I ARRIVED at the hospital, I was placed in another cubicle, but still without medication or change of bandages. Soon another officer from the Ontario PD came in and questioned me about what seemed like every unsolved robbery in Ontario during my adult lifetime. There was indeed one other robbery I had committed in Ontario, but at first I continued to deny everything except the attempted robbery that had gotten me shot.

After what seemed like hours of interrogation—I'm sure it wasn't that long—without any medication or treatment for my hand, I saw the police speaking with one of the doctors. The doctor came in, examined my hand, and left. Still no medication, still in pain. Soon the doctor came back in. "Are you left-handed or right-handed?"

Hmm, what was he implying?

My mind immediately went to amputation.

"Your left hand is seriously injured and in danger of infection. We're thinking of taking it."

"I'm right-handed. Could you send the officer back in?"

When the officer returned, I told him about the other liquor store robbery in Ontario. He took notes and turned me back over to the doctor.

I was taken out of the emergency room and immediately prepped for surgery. I began to say the Twenty-third Psalm, "The Lord is my shepherd…"

PSALM 23

The Lord is my shepherd, I shall not want.
He maketh me to lie down in green pastures:
he leadeth me beside the still waters.
He restoreth my soul:
he leadeth me in the paths of righteousness
for his name's sake.
Yea, though I walk
through the valley of the shadow of death,
I will fear no evil:
for thou art with me;
thy rod and thy staff
they comfort me.
Thou preparest a table before me
in the presence of mine enemies:
thou anointest my head with oil;
my cup runneth over.
Surely goodness and mercy shall follow me
all the days of my life:
and I will dwell in the house of the Lord
for ever.

Because I wasn't fasting, they did not put me completely under during the surgery. I was in a semiconscious state throughout, and I can recall hearing some of the comments the attendants made as they worked on my hand. Things like, "Well, he won't be using this hand to rob anymore."

I can recall having to pee really bad. I told the nurse beside me, and she helped me out with a bedside urinal. I looked into her eyes. "I would really love a Baby Ruth candy bar."

She smiled. "That's the first time I've heard that during a surgery."

But the thing that stuck with me was how the surgeons joked about whether I would be robbing anyone else in the future. There were snickers and giggling all around. Fortunately for me the surgeon's work was superb, and it led to them saving my hand in spite of my crime.

After I finally drifted off to sleep, I was abruptly awakened by a policeman who asked my identity extremely loudly and dropped what I later found out was a warrant for my arrest concerning the first Ontario robbery.

I dozed again, but was later awakened by my federal probation officer. He was there regarding the federal probation I had received ending my employment with the IRS. I don't recall what exactly I said to him, but I had violated my probation.

"I'm really sorry to see all that has happened to you," he said. We had developed a relationship over the months, and I could feel the sincerity in his comments.

The third visitor I received that morning was the nurse who assisted in my surgery. She handed me a Baby Ruth. "In all my years of nursing, I have never seen a man in so much trouble ask for a candy bar, of all things." She smiled and left.

GOD'S PLAN IS ALWAYS GRAND

"For I know the thoughts that I think toward you, saith the Lord, thoughts of peace, and not of evil, to give you an expected end."
Jeremiah 29:11

WHEN I FINALLY woke up I realized this wasn't a dream. I was indeed under arrest, in the hospital, shackled to the bed by my ankle. It was the beginning of the first day of my incarceration.

I had prayed to God about getting me out of my situation. This, however, was not the way I expected. I think deep down I realized God had a plan; at least, I truly believed He had my best interests in mind.

The embarrassment of falling that far that fast hadn't hit me yet. But there were still emotions that caused me to question God and His methods.

However, the fourth visitor I had was the most important. I can't remember his name or even his face, I only remember he was a man of God. Perhaps an angel.

"I'm the hospital chaplain. Could I pray for you?"

I said yes.

He began to pray.

I don't remember what he prayed or how he prayed, I only

remember being overwhelmed by an intense feeling of remorse, which was soon overcome by a great joy. I threw up a lot. I don't know why. Maybe the medication, the food, or my excitement at the experience I was going through in that moment. Seemed like the vomiting wasn't going to stop, but it did, and then came the Gift.

I began to speak words that sounded like nonsense to the human ear. God had taken control of my tongue. I have since learned that I spoke a heavenly language and that this is evidence of the indwelling of God's Spirit in man. People in the past had tried to coach me to do this on my own, but this was the real deal.

The chaplain called for attendants to clean up the mess I had made, but I continued to speak in tongues. Immediately following this came Peace. The Bible calls it "the peace of God, which passeth all understanding" (Philippians 4:7). I can only agree and attest to the fact that it was this Peace that preserved me throughout the tremendous ordeal I was headed for. This Peace continues to keep me centered in my life today. It may not come immediately, but it takes over when I settle down and realize who is really in control, when I realize whose I am.

For those who may not believe or who are on the border, please don't stop. God became real in my life on that pivotal day, September 24, 1985. He was real all along, but like many, I didn't accept Him as such. As you take this journey with me, my prayer is that you too will be convinced that there is a God. He's there for all of us.

WHAT ABOUT YOU?

Maybe you're saying, "I want that peace! Why not me!? Why don't I have the Holy Spirit?"

Are you really ready for him? Would you rather be in prison with Jesus than with the Boss-Man who keeps you alive for a pack of cigarettes? Have you prayed yet for God to step in and help you out of your situation and have you told him you never want to go back?

It works like this: "Thou shalt find him, if thou seek him with all thy heart and with all thy soul." (Deuteronomy 4:29)

That's what I did and you can do it too.

GETTING ACQUAINTED

Incarceration in the county jail hospital ward can be misleading. It is incarceration, but it really wasn't all that bad.

My roommate was a younger black man named James who had experience in the jail system. He had also been arrested for robbery. According to him, during his attempted getaway the sheriff's deputies cornered him when he tripped running up a hillside adjacent to the freeway. He said one of the deputies shot him in the groin while he was down. Truth or fiction, I don't know. I do know he had been shot. He was my first introduction to the jail system. He talked about me vomiting and said he thought I wasn't going to stop. He never mentioned the chaplain or me speaking in tongues and unfortunately, neither did I.

On my previous trips to the jails I had been on the other side of lockdown, and I had a hard time adjusting to the fact that I was an inmate. The voices of the nurses and medical staff throughout the day brought a sense of normalcy to my predicament. Hot meals were brought at appropriate times. We even got to pick from a menu.

For the most part, the doctors and nurses treated me like any other patient. The one clear reminder was my ankle being shackled to the bed. When we had to use the restroom both feet were shackled together, and we were escorted by the deputy.

In the evening, when the hallways cleared, the night deputy would shackle our feet together and allow us to come out of the room and watch a small TV he brought in. The picture was horrible, but the sound was okay.

James talked of his past life of crime and plans for future ways to make money by selling drugs. I talked about my life with the IRS. Although I had been away from the job for over a year, I had little else to speak about. My drug use did not lead to friends or relationships to speak of. I could only recall the names of dealers or those who ran the crack houses.

Although I talked a lot to James, I really felt more connected to the deputy. It seemed that James and I had little in common other than our current situation. Both James and the deputy warned me that when I actually got to the county jail, I needed to leave the law enforcement stuff behind. I was so naïve.

I had heard stories and seen movies about what happens to law enforcement people who find themselves behind bars, but I guess I still hadn't accepted the facts. I didn't even realize how serious a crime robbery was until speaking with James.

Although I had worked in law enforcement for ten years—thirteen counting my internship—that was federal law enforcement, and there was a big difference between federal and state law. Not only that, but the crimes I investigated were generally violations of federal tax laws: failure to file, filing a false return, filing multiple returns, and so on.

James told me how many years I could be facing. Years? That had never dawned on me.

The deputy even suggested that I "PC up," which meant requesting protective custody. I'd never thought about that. To be honest, I never thought about it after that, either.

I had been raised under difficult circumstances and felt I could handle pretty much anything. The jail couldn't be that bad, could it?

I would find out soon enough.

During my first couple of days in the hospital I was allowed to place a call. I called the uncle who lived across the street from my mom. For some reason, I couldn't get through on her phone. My uncle told me my mother knew what had happened. Naturally, she was devastated.

This was the news I dreaded the most. My life was now exposed and my mother, the one person in the world I least wanted to hurt, was hurt to the max.

She was so proud of how I had turned out, knowing the odds were against both of us in the projects. College, the IRS, it all seemed like a fairy tale.

But my life was in the process of crumbling, and knowing her, she had seen it coming long before I did.

MOMS

I HAVE TO DEDICATE this chapter to the one who made it all possible, my mother. There were other moms in my life, but none compared to her. She was always there for me. As time went on, she was there for my kids and later she was there for my kids' kids.

At the time of my arrest, my kids and I were staying with her because I had lost our home in foreclosure due to the drugs. We initially rented a house across the street from her, but that house went into foreclosure as well. I had stopped paying rent as soon as I found out the landlord was in trouble, and we stayed there as long as we could. I had applied for county assistance, but found out that the kids' mom was already receiving a check for them. She apparently intercepted the mail before the mailman made it to our house, knowing that checks came out on the first and the fifteenth of every month—Mother's Day, they called it.

Because I was terminated for cause, I didn't qualify for unemployment. I had actually been given the opportunity to resign, which I did, but this didn't make any difference. Naturally, I was upset at the time, because I felt I had contributed my share in taxes and unemployment insurance.

During the one-and-a-half years of my unemployment, I found it difficult to apply for entry-level positions. Hey, I was a college graduate with thirteen years of experience in law enforcement. However, my record precluded me from getting anything in that field. Even though theft of government property is a misdemeanor, it's a crime of moral turpitude, and employers frown on that. I didn't have the skills or the desire to work on labor-driven jobs.

But my mom was there, as always. She took me and the kids and our dog into her home. I was still able to get food stamps, and during tax season I did a few returns, but my pride and my addiction held me back.

Mother was the steadying force. Even though she raised me by herself, I never considered myself a "mama's boy." I think she nick-named me Butch because that name seemed to be a sign of strength back in those days, and she wanted people to know I was all boy.

She and my dad officially divorced when I was around two years old. I don't remember him ever living with us. I later found out that after he graduated from college he went into the service and fought during the Korean conflict. By the time I was old enough to remember him he had already remarried.

For a while mom and I lived with her parents in the Ross Township and West View area of Pittsburgh. My grandfather had built the home with the help of his sons. It included a lot of land, grass, and trees. The nearest neighbors were yards apart. It was basically within a forest, what we would call country living. There were fruit trees, ponds, and creeks. It was a boy's dream, and I later took advantage of it whenever we went back to visit. It was definitely big enough for my mom and I, and she was the only girl, but for some reason she made a decision to move. It was this independence that was passed on to me as I grew up.

So it was just me and my mom. We moved out of my grandparents' home before I started kindergarten. I had gone to a nursery school since I was two, so school was no big deal for me.

We moved to the Hill District, into the projects. Now this was totally the opposite of grandma's house, but at the time I was too young to realize it. West View was pretty much all white, except for the small section of homes where my grandparents lived. Most of the neighbors were either family relatives or longtime friends.

"The Hill," on the other hand, was without a doubt all black. So black that even milkmen and taxi cabs refused to come into the area.

When I was very little, my mother spent a great deal of time reading to me or reciting stories, like "The Three Little Bears" and "The Boy Who Cried Wolf." She made sure my homework was done, although I was blessed to have a mind to which reading and math came easy. She also introduced me to the library, so I and several friends spent hours reading and checking out books on our favorite subjects, usually sports or World War II stories.

I don't remember my mother ever cussing. When we walked to her best friend's apartment, she might have a beer, but that was about it. She did smoke cigarettes though. As far as church goes, we were sort of hit or miss in our neighborhood. However, because I spent so many weekends at the home of my grandmother, who was definitely one of the most Christian ladies I ever met, I went to Sunday school and church with her.

My mother was a very attractive woman. She had me when she was twenty years old, so I imagine there were men beating down the door to get to her. I can honestly say I never recall waking up in our apartment and a strange man being there. In fact, during our first several years in the projects we only had one bedroom, and my mom and I shared the bed. We didn't have a car and my mother didn't drive until I was in my late teens. We caught the trolley or walked everywhere we went.

For a long time she sold Avon Products to make ends meet. She also worked in the same warehouse as one of my uncles and my grandmother. There was an older woman next door who I came to call Aunt Lila, or YaYa, who babysat me. As I got older she sort of watched over me. She kept the key to the apartment, and when I got home from school I would get it from her and go to our apartment and watch TV and do homework. By the time I was seven or eight, I began riding the trolley by myself and would spend many weekends with my grandparents. If my mother had to work over-time, she would call and give me instructions on how to cook a TV dinner or pot pie.

My mom began to sleep on the couch as I grew, and when I reached nine or ten we moved into a two-bedroom apartment.

I spent a lot of time alone in the apartment, but when I went out-side there were plenty of kids to play with. I was light-skinned and an only child, so I do remember getting into quite a few fights. I was well liked by the girls, but hated by a lot of the boys. I even remember having to pay one kid a nickel a week as "protection dues," although the only thing it protected me from was him pounding on me. I never told my mom about these things.

The projects were teeming with kids, all ages, all sizes, and all black, like the rest of the Hill District. My grandparents and mom pampered me since I was the only child, and I got more than my share of toys at Christmas and birthdays. I always seemed to have a quarter or something in my pocket for candy or the ice cream truck.

I spent a lot of time running from other boys, so in some way I think it helped me in sports, especially track. My mother made sure to try to attend every open house or special event at school. She even saved old report cards dating back to elementary school. But one thing my mom couldn't do was attend my sporting events. It would have been nearly impossible for her, because they were always held during the daytime and she would have had to miss work. This con-tinued throughout high school, where I was pretty much a star foot-ball player and earned a college scholarship.

Over the years, I developed a lot of friendships. When I began playing football, most of the team became my band of brothers. Because the team was fairly small for a city league football team, we usually began summer practice with fewer than twenty-five guys, so there was a special bond between us. There's something about sacri-fice and going through various ordeals together that bring the par-ticipants closer together.

Official summer practice lasted for two weeks, but it was a grueling two weeks. We ran so much in the heat that we actually drank each other's sweat, mixed in with the towels soaked in water that were brought out to us periodically. As long as it was wet, we didn't mind the salty taste. This was before the days of health experts emphasizing hydration for football players in the heat. These were the guys I spent much of my time with. During the summer and fall most of this time was spent on the football field.

Throughout the year we would go to parties and social events together. During the off season, we would work out together. Some of us were multisport athletes; track and volleyball were our favorites.

Yet I had many friends outside football who I continued to hang out with. Unfortunately, this group included most of the guys I joined smoking cigarettes and marijuana, and drinking beer and wine. All of these activities were no-nos for athletes, so most of it was kept secret from all but my closest friends on the teams.

Even then I was leading a double life.

Many of my childhood friendships continue until today. My mother always welcomed my friends. I think she knew friends were important to me as an only child.

As I got older, my mom being at work, and me being home alone, made my house a great meeting place for me and the fellas. It was one place we could go with no adult supervision. We played games, talked about girls, even getting up the courage to call them on occasion, and watched television.

My mother instilled in me a sense of respect and love that never left me. Not only my mother, but my grandmothers on both sides insisted that I address adults as "sir" or "ma'am." I can remember one occasion when I was in my earlier teens that I cursed at one of the project mothers. When she later called my mother and spilled the beans, it was the worst feeling I could ever have. Mom cried, and so did I, and I promised it would never happen again.

It never did.

Cussing or any type of foul language was forbidden in my house when mom was home. She and I didn't even use words such as "fart" around each other. When I heard friends use these types of words in front of their moms, I was surprised, because it was so ingrained in me that I assumed no one did it.

Another forbidden topic in the house was anything involving sex. Everything I learned beginning at puberty was what I learned from the street. If I had grown up on a farm, you could say I lived a very sheltered life, but I lived where I lived and sex was a big topic. I didn't get the official "birds and bees" conversation until my high school graduation day, and it was my father, who had come to see me graduate, who gave it to me. No doubt my mom had told him it was long overdue. Unfortunately, it was over six months after I had become sexually active with a girl who later became my first wife. At the time of my talk with dad, I later found out, she was already pregnant with our first child.

My mother had done a great job of keeping our home as pure as she possibly could. As I mentioned earlier, there were never any men coming over—that is, until my junior year in high school.

"Ray," who was soon to be my stepfather, began spending time at our home, and I hated it. I felt like the bond between my mom and I was broken. He even started to spend the night—sleeping on the couch, not in my mother's room. I still felt our privacy was being invaded.

He did have a car, and that allowed us to go places like the drive-in or my grandparents' home, but I still didn't like him.

They married after a few months of dating, and we moved into my grandparent's home. I was devastated. I was at the wedding, but I made sure that on moving day, I was in Cleveland with my father and his family. My father didn't help matters much, always instilling in me that a person could have only one father and he was mine. It's amazing how interested in me he seemed to become after mom remarried, which was over fifteen years after their divorce.

My mother was my protector. I didn't have problems with school or grades, so she didn't have to worry about that. I had my share of fights and being chased home when I was younger, but I kept that to myself, so she had no worries there either, although there were many times I came through the door at a very high speed and if it had been locked, I might have gotten beat down right in the hallway. She questioned why I was out of breath, but didn't go much further. Perhaps she knew and figured that somehow it would be resolved.

Once I got older and started playing football in high school, the street chasing and street fights stopped. Guys realized that if they messed with me they were messing with the whole team, and they didn't want that. My mom had little interest in sports and I did those well, so she had no problems in that area either. I'm sure her major concern was getting me out of the environment without a criminal record.

In 1968, when rioting broke out over Martin Luther King's assassination, my neighborhood immediately went up in flames. My mother, who was at work, called me at home and pretty much put me on "house arrest." I reluctantly obeyed.

After Mom came home, during this period of lockdown, I asked her for a cigarette. She gave me one and immediately called her best friend and told her I had finally admitted to smoking. All of that hiding ashtrays and airing out the house had been for naught. She had known all along.

After a day or so I convinced her to let me out. The schools were closed. As long as I stayed in the projects, I was safe. She agreed and told me that under no circumstances was I to bring anything home that was taken in the looting that was going on.

I disobeyed this order, though, when I found out the local dry cleaners was being looted—she and I had clothes there. I went with a group of friends to the cleaners. As luck would have it, I spotted someone running with what looked like our clothes. I immediately grabbed them. Sure enough, some of the stuff they had was ours.

The brother had so much that he didn't quibble about giving me my London Fog trench coat and her dresses. I took them home. When mom got home from work, after she fussed me out for disobeying, she admitted that she was grateful our stuff had been retrieved.

She and I survived the days of rioting. Helicopters flew overhead, and the National Guard drove up and down the streets, but the projects were a safe haven for my friends and me.

My mother made a point of questioning me about any strange "friends" I brought into the house. She was very familiar with the kids I had gone to school with all the way from kindergarten to high school, and she knew most of their mothers. But if an odd duck showed up, she picked up on it immediately. She didn't mind asking who they were, where they lived and how old they were.

My mother knew that I talked to girls a lot on the phone. She didn't get into my relationships with them. There was even a time when my girlfriend and I were honored at Pitt Stadium along with other high schoolers. I had been selected Scholar Athlete of the Year and she was the high school beauty queen. It wasn't until our picture appeared in the local black newspaper, *The Pittsburgh Courier*, that my mom was even aware. For some reason I kept things like this to myself. A couple of times neighbors told her about girls being at the house, but I explained it away by saying they were talking about my cousin who, with her brother, spent a lot of time with me.

Mom's prayers, my overall upbringing, and just plain luck allowed me to almost escape that all-too-familiar trap for young blacks in situations similar to mine. However, there was another mother who had aspirations similar to my mom's concerning the oldest girl among her thirteen kids.

I learned to call her mom too. The oldest girl was to later become my wife and the mother of my first three children. When I mention her, I speak of her as my children's mother, because that is the only place she has in my story. She was never really a wife, and I don't know that she knew how to be.

Her mother was a wonderful lady, a devout Catholic even though she had had these thirteen children out of wedlock. As time passed, I realized she was looking out for her daughter's best interest.

I was graduating from high school and on my way to college on a football scholarship. I see now that she saw me as a ticket to get her daughter out of the hood, just like my mother was working to see me get clear of the environment.

I spent a lot of time at their house. It felt so unusual being around so many kids. I soon became part of the family. Mom allowed me to spend the night whenever I felt like it. I was seventeen, my girlfriend was fifteen, but it was as if we were already married. There's not much else to say. She told me she was pregnant before she actually was. I fell for that. We continued our intimacy and pretty soon she really was pregnant. Mom had always treated me as one of her own. When we broke the news of her daughter's pregnancy she rejoiced and began making plans for the baby.

I believe my mother got wind of the girl from the North Side of Pittsburgh sooner than I thought. Because my mother had moved us into my grandmother's house once she got married, I was outside our school district. This was the summer before my senior year in high school, and there was no way I was going to transfer to another school. I used my best friend's address and spent the night at his house on many occasions, but there were times I stayed on the North Side.

My mother knew there was a girl involved, and I could tell in her voice when I would call and say that it was too late or that there was some type of early event at school that she doubted my explanations. I eventually introduced Pam to my family, and she came over to visit a few times. One night it snowed so bad the buses stopped running, and she was stuck there with us.

My grandmother reluctantly allowed her to stay, but made several trips up the stairs to the bedrooms to ensure everyone was in their right place.

Pam's mom, on the other hand, made a big deal out of her pregnancy and introduced us to her friends as if we were already married. I didn't tell my mother about the pregnancy until about two months after I found out, right before I left for college. I could tell my mother was heartbroken.

However, my mother made it clear that as long as I was underage, there was no way she would sign for me to marry. It wasn't until

I found out a second child was on the way that my mother agreed for me to marry. I later found out that Pam had lied; there was no second child on the way at that time. But it was too late. The wedding happened when my daughter was seven months old.

My third mom was my stepmother. There have been many negative stories about stepmothers, and mine fit the bill. From my childhood until adulthood, she treated me like the stepchild in a storybook. When I visited my dad and family during the summer, I did most of the chores. Actually, I did all the chores. I washed the dishes, took all the clothes to the Laundromat, and one time was even given the assignment of scrubbing the bathroom tile grout with a toothbrush.

I learned very early that there was a big difference between my stepbrothers and me. She had done all she could to spend money that should have been earmarked for me and my mother when I was growing up. My father provided little to no support for us. When I visited during the summer, there was a chance I might come home with some school clothes. That was about it, other than birthdays and Christmas, when he would send something.

The one thing my stepmother did in my favor was trying to block the marriage between me and my pregnant girlfriend. She saw things as they really were and spent hours trying to convince me that having a baby out of wedlock was not the worst thing that could happen. She was a social worker and seemed to know the ropes with families like my girlfriend's. However, I couldn't be convinced.

Over the years, my stepmother and I became very close. When I graduated from college and went on to work with the government, she somehow had a change of heart. Later in life, during a bad period I was going through, she opened the doors to her home, and I flew from California to Cleveland to stay with her. My dad was seldom home, and she and I spent hours talking. I found out she was really a very intelligent woman, as close to a genius as I'd ever met.

During that period, I realized she had become more of a mother to me. We talked about our mistakes in life, she giving me the woman's point of view. She gave me advice I cherish even now. I could never replace my brothers, and I understand that, but she finally gave me everything that perhaps a stepmother could—life's experiences from her point of view.

I guess most women have that motherly instinct that separates them from their male counterparts. These three women had a big impact on me. Their backgrounds were very different. The choices they made in life were different also.

As I said earlier, my true mom stopped living her life and began living mine it seems from the moment I was born. No one could replace her, no one would probably want to. She embodies what the Proverbs say: "Who can find a virtuous woman? for her price is far above rubies.... Her children arise up, and call her blessed" (Proverbs 31:10, 28 KJV).

I mention the others because looking back, I understand where they were coming from and what they sought to accomplish. My grandmothers were also there for me. I could write chapters on the lessons I learned from them, but I'll leave that for another time.

THIS IS IT

WHEN I FIRST arrived at the county jail, it was way worse than I expected, and that's an understatement. Richard Pryor, after his time in jail, said something like, I've been to prison and all I can say is thank God for prisons, because there's some crazy people up in there. Not a direct quote, but that was the gist of it.

I spent about two weeks in the hospital's jail ward. I had pretty much been pampered, fed, operated on a few times and now, ready or not, was on my way to the real deal. A couple of deputies picked a few of us up and took us the short distance to the jail. We arrived in our pajamas and were immediately greeted by the other inmates as we marched through the bars and into a holding cell.

Listening to the conversations of the guys who came in with me, I deduced that most had already been in the jail and had been out for hospital procedures. I was one of the few who hadn't been indoctrinated yet.

Not long after the bars closed, an earthquake struck. I remember thinking, *Thank you, Jesus, I may get delivered like the apostle Paul.*

No such luck.

I was given the one phone call and called my mom and told her how crazy everyone seemed. I'm sure she could hear the anguish in my voice as she tried to comfort me, saying I was the type that could get along with anybody. I held back tears, realizing this was it. The hospital was just a temporary rest stop. Rest was over. It was now time to put up or shut up. I decided to shut up.

It seemed like hours, and it probably was, before my name was called. I was taken into a separate office and asked about gang affiliations, medications, and the like. Once again, I couldn't keep my mouth shut about the IRS. The officer passed over that piece of information as if he had just been audited. I could see that I was on this side and he was on another.

I was given a blanket, sheet, and pillow, and then I was escorted to the jail's infirmary. The pajamas drew the attention of every cell block I passed, and the catcalls were endless.

SICK AND INSANE

J AMES HAD BEAT me there. He greeted me and introduced me to the unit's shot caller, a Mexican with a Native American heritage who was called Geronimo. There was an empty bed, which I later learned was not to be taken for granted.

Due to my surgeries, my hand was in a cast.

Geronimo asked where I was from and what my crime was.

Usually these were the first two of three questions asked. You might be asked your name. When I told him Pomona, I found out we had that in common. The crime, armed robbery, was something that was looked up to by inmates. The fact that I had been shot was another plus.

Geronimo even had a homie who had tried a robbery with a pellet gun and got the gun enhancement dropped because it wasn't a real gun. Fortunately me and Geronimo hit it off right from the start. Even more fortunately, James hadn't mentioned my indiscretions as a federal agent. That would have been the death blow for me.

Life in the infirmary wasn't all that bad. It was as if God watched over me. People say God won't put more on you than you can bear. It seemed as if I was getting baby bites of the system, until I was ready to handle the meatier aspects of being an inmate.

We had our own eating area, which included a TV. Geronimo determined what we watched. He didn't much care for sports, especially football or basketball, but at times he would give in after proving that he had the authority not to. We watched mostly soap operas or old re-runs.

The food was brought to us by a deputy with other inmates from the kitchen. Sometimes it was hot, but most times it was cold. I don't know if I ever slept as much as I did during this period of my life. Sleeping made the time go faster.

In the early morning, about 4 or 5 a.m., a deputy would come in and announce who was on the movement list. Usually this meant you were scheduled for court, but sometimes it meant something else, like a transfer to another county, going out for a medical appointment, or "catching the chain," which met going to the big house—the state penitentiary.

The infirmary sat right outside the one-man cells provided for people who were on some sort of special watch, usually suicidal or with some sort of mental problem. One young man, Gene, was in one of these cells. I'm not sure what his problem was, if indeed he actually had one. Two or three times a week, the deputy would bring Gene into our unit so he could watch TV.

I soon found out that he could braid hair, and once I got money on the books, I'd buy him something from the canteen in payment for him braiding my hair. Gene was really a character. He told me that every now and then he played crazy so they would take him to Patton State Hospital. He liked going there because the men and women were on the same floor. He spent most of his time figuring out ways to make it into a woman's room to have sex. He told me one story of a woman who walked the hallways with her right arm and hand pointed straight up as if it were some kind of salute. Gene told me that when he was finally able to make his way to her room, she kept the arm pointed up during their entire sexual encounter.

The men in the single-man rooms who were believed to be mentally ill or suicide threats were not given clothes. They wore paper gowns. When an officer came with their food it was given to them through a slot in the door. The guards never opened the door alone.

A couple of months after I met Gene, an officer was walking past his room and Gene called out to him. For some reason the officer, probably a rookie, opened the door. Gene pulled the man into the room and beat up on him.

When the guys in the infirmary noticed what was going on, there was a lot of hooting and hollering in favor of Gene. There was no one to assist the officer. After a few minutes, Gene came running out of the room naked. He dashed into the hallway and out of our sight.

It wasn't long before the deputy came out, and we heard over the loudspeaker "officer down." Within another few minutes we saw several officers dragging Gene, kicking and screaming, back to his room.

They shut the door and began beating him. We could hear his screams and their comments throughout the fight. He took a bad beating, but not so bad for him to be placed in with us.

I didn't see Gene for a good while after that. When he was let back in to watch TV with us, he didn't talk much about his scuffle with the jailers.

His last words to me after I had been sentenced were to be careful when I got to the state prison. He told me it was different there, and that I should be sure to hang with blacks and especially not Mexicans. Until then, while in the county jail, I pretty much hadn't thought of any racial bias, although I did notice that many Mexicans referred to blacks in a derogatory manner when they spoke in Spanish.

I didn't get to know most of the guys who came through the infirmary, but several of us were there for months. One was having psych evaluations due to a mental disorder. He was a huge brother, and few—if anyone—wanted to mess with him. The two of us talked a lot about the Bible, trying to prove or disapprove its legitimacy: was it really a holy book, given to others to write through inspiration of God? We wondered how God communicated with the its writers. For some reason we both felt special to God—me because of the shooting and he because his grandmother told him so.

We spent time in the book of Hosea and felt that our wives were examples of Gomer in her infidelity to her husband. He had been arrested after dousing his wife with gasoline on a crowded bus. He told stories of her using his kids to get at him. The wife wouldn't let him see them after they were separated.

While they were together she had received welfare checks while he worked, and when she was caught, the county began attaching his paycheck as repayment for money he never saw. She was unfaithful and didn't mind throwing that up in his face, either. She had even told him to come and get the kids and when he did, she called the police and claimed it was a kidnapping.

It wasn't long after he got bailed out on that charge that he asked to meet her on a public bus. He said that once he emptied the mayonnaise jar full of gasoline on her and lit her up with a match, everyone on the bus, including the driver, made a hasty escape. The damage he did to her was permanent. Geronimo said it was probably better than killing her, since every time she looked at her chest she would think of him. His crime was sensationalized in the newspaper; rightly so, and whenever he went to court he said there were lots of reporters who followed the case.

Another man I came to know was blind. He sold cocaine in a town in the high desert. He could tell who you were by your footsteps. I thought his bust very comical in that he was arrested after selling to two undercover officers. Since he was blind, nobody actually needed to be undercover.

Before he went totally blind due to his diabetes, he would periodically lose his sight and regain it. One time he and a friend had picked up two women who they spent the weekend with. They planned to go on a picnic that Sunday, so they all went to the grocery store before the picnic. As he and his lady friend were at the meat counter, he was feeling the steaks to see how thick they were. As he fumbled with the steak, his vision cleared. He looked up at the lady he was with and claimed she was one of the ugliest women he had ever seen. He quickly made up an excuse as to why he couldn't go to the picnic.

He later gave his friend a long chewing out about allowing him to embarrass himself in front of all of his homeboys, since he was supposed to be a big baller in that city. We all had a big laugh about that one.

A lot of guys came in and out. One older man must have been arrested ten to fifteen times just during the period I was there. He was an alcoholic, and all of his arrests were for being drunk in public. He told stories of times that even the police would buy him a bottle and later on arrest him for being drunk.

Another young man became known as Kibbles and Bits because during a commercial burglary, the police showed up. He tried to hide, but they let a police dog loose. The dog soon found him, and they apparently let him chew on this guy for quite some time before pulling the dog off.

Another young man came in who was obviously gay. I noticed that after a few days he began sleeping in the same bunk as Geronimo. One of the officers questioned it, but it didn't go any further than that. This young man would often be in the shower as well, with one man after another coming in with him. I had long since learned to keep my eyes, ears, and mouth to myself. That information was general knowledge within the dorm, but that's as far as it went.

James became popular due to the damage done to his private area. He retold the shooting story over and over again. Sometimes, gay guys would come into the infirmary after getting their meds outside the dorm, just to see James's private parts. They would even pay him. I never asked to look, so I don't know what the big deal was, but he reached celebrity status.

Soon James was transferred out of the infirmary to one of the other cell blocks. Based on what I heard from inmates who came into our dorm after being beaten up, the "Man down, J Block" announcements over the loudspeaker, and the sounds of officers' footsteps making their way into the fray, I figured I was best off where I was. It was another way God was looking out for me. With my hand the way it was, it would have been pretty hard to protect myself.

One guy who came in obviously didn't fit in. Everyone knew he was a wimp, and when he got to go to the canteen, he didn't stand a chance.

His only protection was Geronimo, who took most of his change as protection dues and mostly talked others out of bothering the guy.

As usual, I talked to everyone, and on a few occasions I had struck up a conversation with this young man. I talked to him about the Bible and how God had purpose in our lives.

The night before he was released, someone strong-armed his tennis shoes. He didn't say anything, but not long after he left one of the deputies escorted me to an office. He asked if I knew this guy, and I responded that I did.

He asked me about the tennis shoes.

"I hadn't really noticed what type of shoes he had on."

The deputy accused me of covering up. "He says you're the only one on the unit who would probably tell us who has the shoes."

I stuck to my story.

Another deputy came in. "I know your background. Maybe I could ask the judge to go lighter on your sentence."

I told him the charges against me.

He kind of backed off about the sentencing. "Do it for morality's sake."

I refused. "Consider my situation."

"I understand," the deputy said, and that was it.

When I got back to the dorm, some of the guys asked me what they had wanted. I told them the truth, that somehow they felt me and the guy were friends and I would help him get his shoes back. I told them what I had told the deputies: I didn't know anything about any shoes. That was one of the obvious codes of this jungle called jail.

Being in the infirmary had its privileges. One was the use of the pay phone. Because there were only a few of us in there, perhaps fifteen to twenty at the most, there were hardly any fights over whose turn it was to use the phone. Back then, one could still call out collect and even to call without reversing the charges was only twenty cents.

However, the longer I was there the less I wanted to make phone calls. When I made calls I only found out about things I had no control over. My oldest son sneaking out of the house, or the youngest being sweet-talked by his mother and letting her into the house, which was a definite no-no as far as my mom was concerned, and for all the right reasons.

Visits were also easier to get, because in the infirmary, we were hardly ever on lockdown. But visits became more of a chore and brought more heartache than I wanted. I would see my mom and the kids and grandkid and just want to cry. I wanted so much to be with them. These were all no-contact visits. You spoke via telephone and saw them through glass. After a while, visiting was no fun at all.

One time the kids' mother came, too. She talked to me about how she had changed and kept standing up to show off her shape. What was that all about? I guess she was trying to prove to me that she was no longer a crackhead and had put on some weight. If she only knew how much I felt our roles should have been reversed.

God, life just ain't fair sometimes. But what did I know. In the end we win, speaking of saved folk, and I was on my way to victory.

All of us long-termers had chores to do. If the dorm was judged clean by the deputies, it improved our standing about when we would be fed. It really didn't matter too much for us, because we usually didn't go anywhere to eat. The food was brought into the lunchroom. However, if we were at or near the top of the list, there was a better chance of getting hot meals. It meant a lot to the other dorms, because it determined what order they would be called for chow.

I chose to clean the toilets and urinals. I think I made this choice as part of my own self-punishment for getting myself in this situation. It was a job no one wanted, but I took it. I believe I was in a frame of mind where pride didn't matter anymore.

Later in life, living as a Christian, I realized that this was a step in helping me put pride in its proper place. As Scripture says, "Humble yourselves in the sight of the Lord, and He shall lift you up" (James 4:10).

I never thought I would be there, but there I was, sitting on toilets doing my business while everyone was around. I had seen this when I had taken prisoners to the jail myself. It was the one thing I said I could never do. You'd be surprised what you can do when the time comes to do it. I sat there like everyone else. When people said flush, I flushed. No worries.

BUS BOYS

IF THERE WAS a part of being locked up that I really hated, it was being transported to and from court. People may think this wouldn't be all that bad, being able to be outside and seeing the sights of the real world. It was the bus itself.

In general, whenever we went to court, or if there happened to be a transfer to another jail, we rode a bus. To begin with, you're awakened in the wee hours of the morning, usually around 4 a.m. You're taken to breakfast and then moved to a holding tank, which depended upon your destination.

We were herded into this cell like cattle. There was nowhere to sit except the toilet, so everyone stood. If for some reason you had to back up and stepped on someone's shoes, that would probably lead to the threat of a fight.

To crowd that many people, criminals or not, into such small places for extended periods of time is inhuman. At times we stood for an hour or so, waiting for the deputies to get to our cell and call our name.

Once your name is called, you make your way through the horde and into the hallway, where the deputies handcuff your wrist to someone else's. Because of the cast on my left hand, I was always cuffed by my right.

Depending on your crime or your destination, your feet could also be shackled, but in general, going to court you were just cuffed by your hand to that of some unfamiliar person whose name was alphabetically next to yours.

Once a busload was all attached, we were marched out onto the bus. The interior of the bus was divided by an iron gate, which kept the regular inmates in their place, but also gave space to anyone in protective custody so they wouldn't be exposed to the others. Any women in lockup would also ride in front of the gate.

Guys loved to sit in the front seats of the rear inmate section, because there they could heckle the PCs.

If they had a cigarette or two, and were fortunate enough to sit right at the gate separating the men from the women, they could buy a quick feel or get a woman to expose a breast or something. That would naturally bring hoots and hollers throughout the bus, and those of us toward the back knew something crazy had happened. I would just shut my eyes and wish I were somewhere else. Anywhere else.

I guess I hated the bus rides so much because they reminded me of whose side I was now on. There was a distinct difference between us and the guards. The shackles and iron gates reminded me of that. Not to mention that the more the inmates acted like animals, the more I tended to agree that we were indeed animals. The shouting and hollering would nearly drive me insane.

If I was fortunate enough to have a window to look out of, I would try to look out. The windows, though, put me in another predicament, because as you rode through the streets or on the freeway, you would catch the stares of those riding or walking by. The big letters across both sides of the bus—San Bernardino County Sheriff's Department—the black and white colors and the bars on the windows might as well have said Ringling Brothers' Circus. I felt as if we were on display.

The other problem with the windows was the fact that the freeways and many of the streets were well known to me. As I watched familiar neighborhoods roll by, the desire to be outside my current situation got worse.

Most courts had a basement entry for the buses. Otherwise, we went in through a back gate. Either way we were marched off the bus after the women and PCs were taken to their holding cells.

Once we got to the holding cells it was more of the same. If we weren't going to court immediately our chains would be undone. The cells were still too small and the inmates usually too many. The noise was constant. How I longed for quiet, but this was not the place to get it. There were fights or threats of fights. If you were unfortunate enough not to be called during the morning session, or if you were told to come back in the afternoon, you would have to stay at the holding cell and eat lunch there, usually a box lunch. Sometimes the holding area had tables, but often there was nowhere to eat and you just had to make do. It was always something cold.

The walk up to the courtroom wasn't bad, but sitting in there could be painful. Again, I think it was the stares of the public that got me the most. This was something I would have to learn to overcome. However, as far as trips outside go, I think the worst was my frequent trips to the hospital.

The hospitals were filled with not only people who worked there, but visitors and other patients as well. As I was being escorted to X-ray or the Orthopedic Department, it was not unusual for a mom or dad to grab their kid and move over against the wall. Many of the medical staff were used to us inmates, but the general public may have been seeing a real live criminal in the flesh for the first time. Believe me, it shocked me more than it did them to see us in those jumpsuits, hands and feet cuffed together, doing that inmate shuffle down the hallway. It was almost comical; but hey, this was me.

Due to the secrecy, most times I was caught by surprise by these "field trips." I'm sure this was done to prevent escape attempts. They didn't want to give us a chance to plan anything with anyone on the outside. It also prevented clandestine meetings between you and a family member or friend, where drugs could be passed or, God forbid, you got a chance to kiss your girlfriend. I can understand all of this, but it still made it difficult to lay through a thirty- to forty-minute MRI scan without being prepared. I remember laying on the bed in the scanning room thinking, I hope I don't have to pee, if I do, what happens then? No nurse to hold my hand or pass me a urine bottle. I'd just be in trouble.

Inmates who had committed crimes against children were in really deep trouble in the jails, and so were law enforcement personnel. Because they were usually kept in protective custody, they were housed separately from the rest of us. However, during times of transportation, these individuals were particularly vulnerable. They had to mingle with the rest of us. Even though they were kept separate, there were still opportunities for someone to get at them. Whenever someone from the general population got a chance, like through the window of a bus or the bars of the cells, they were spit on or disrespected in whatever way possible. All they had to see was that green PC jumpsuit, and inmates who were violent or trying to make a name for themselves would take advantage of any opportunity to get to the PCs.

The high-power prisoners wore red jump suits. They were usually handcuffed and shackled at the ankles even during movement within the jail. They were the shot callers higher up than our little infirmary guy, Geronimo. These guys were usually gang leaders or individuals who had shot a policeman. They were high-risk prisoners whose notoriety proceeded them. If they flew a kite (sent a message), people listened. Due to their reputation they were segregated as well. On the bus, in the dining room, in the holding tanks, where ever they went, they were given the officers' full attention.

BOOKER SAYS . . .

Evil requires attention everywhere it goes because it destroys, it murders, it lies, it cheats, it steals, and it abuses you and others in every way it can. Without putting shackles on it, chaos, fear, and death will rule over you—as it tries to do in the holding tanks and transport busses of our prison system.

*Jesus didn't require attention—**His holiness *attracted* attention**. Thousands followed him to hear Him teach and be healed by Him. When he wanted to be alone, he had to get up extra early to find a place to be by himself and talk to God. Now billions have followed Jesus—not out of fear but because they are attracted to his love, mercy, forgiveness, healing, second chances, and the eternal life he offers to those who want it.*

He lets you choose it.

Who do you want to seek and find in your life? Leaders of chaos and destruction or the Leader of peace and restoration that only Jesus can give you?

Choose today.

The worst bus trip I can recall began when we were sitting outside a courthouse waiting to pick up some inmates at a different court then the one I'd gone to. As we sat inside the bus, many of the windows were opened. There were still bars, so no threat of escape.

However, several deputies were standing around the entrance; one of their kids happened to be with one of them. He couldn't have been more than five years old.

One of the inmates shouted that we should kill the little pig, before he grew up to be like his dad.

I don't even know if the little boy understood what was being said and that it was directed at him.

But the deputies knew. They burst onto the bus and began to question us as to who said it. They threatened us with having to sit on the bus all night until someone admitted it. Then they told us we would miss dinner and worst of all, we would miss canteen. That could be disastrous for anyone with money on their books, especially if they smoked. Cigarette smoking inside California's jails and prisons had not yet been banned.

Still no one spoke up. When we got back to the jail, we were told to strip down to nothing, which was the usual course of things. As the deputies walked up and down the line, we had to bend over exposing our butt and cough. This would cause you to expel contraband you may have gotten hold of and hid there. We went through the drill of lifting our penis and testicles to ensure nothing was hidden in those areas either. We also had to bow our heads and run our fingers through our hair for the same reason. When we had gone through the drill, as we started to pull our pants back up, we were told to stand still just as we were.

Usually the female deputies went in another direction during this part of the re-entry into the jail, I suppose to search the ladies. However, we stood there for so long, that eventually the women deputies were making their way up and down the halls as we stood there baring all. Some didn't mind giving us obvious stares, snickers, or comments as they went by. Some stayed in the area just watching.

We were asked over and over who had made the comment. Finally someone came forward and said it was them, but one of the deputies said he was lying because his voice didn't sound the same. We continued to stand there. Finally it became apparent that no one was going to speak up. We were allowed to go to the dining room. But we didn't make it back in time for canteen.

Because I normally ate in the infirmary where I was housed, my first trip to the dining room didn't come until I had been in the jail system for some time. I can still recall that comical moment. I went through the line with everyone else. You weren't allowed to pick where you sat, you just walked in sync to the next chair at the table. They were long tables, seating about forty to fifty inmates.

As I sat down, I asked someone to pass the salt. Mistake. You were just supposed to say "salt" or "juice" or whatever it was. I eventually got the salt. Everyone was eating with an unbelievable fervency. I wrote it off as more animalistic behavior. I continued my politeness, trying to start up conversations.

A deputy quickly told me, "Shut up."

As I slowly spooned through my food, there was a loud bang at the end of the table. A deputy had come down hard with his fist. That meant we were done. I quickly tried to gobble down more of the food on my plate as I stood in line to leave the kitchen. I got a few more bites before I was told to show the deputy at the end of the line my silverware as I placed it in a container. I quickly dumped the food, set the tray down, and left.

I went hungry that night.

COURTSHIP

ONCE YOU GOT to the courtroom, you sat in the jury box with the other inmates. Usually you were not chained, unless your crime or past history mandated it.

Only after I appeared before the judge did I learn that the Honorable Judge Allen was the "hanging judge." That's what Geronimo called him, after I got back to the jail and told him who it was. Geronimo told me the story of Judge Allen sentencing his own son to a great deal of prison time. This was the same judge Geronimo was assigned to. He was in jail on a murder charge. At first I was stupid enough to believe it, not realizing there was no way some judge's son could stand before his father in court.

I didn't meet my attorney until I got to the courtroom. She was a public defender and showed about as much interest in me as we would normally show a flea. She quickly took me aside and read over my case. At this point, I had already confessed to the crime. I told her I really needed my glasses, which were in the possession of the detectives. It took a few meetings with my attorney to actually build a relationship with her. At one time she described me to the judge as a "well-spoken" man, with little to no criminal history. She was a young white woman and new to her profession, I think. This was good, because I found out she hadn't lost the fire she would need to defend her clients. She still had hope in the system.

I really thought she was fighting for me. She had read over my background, and as she got to know me a little better, I feel I became more than that flea. Early in my case she decided to have a lineup. I kind of thought this was useless, especially since I had confessed. Even more than that, how many others would be in the lineup with a cast on his left hand? I expressed my doubts, but she pretty much said, "Let me be the lawyer."

After the lineup and I was picked right away, she explained that she could use the fact that I was the only one with a cast to my advantage.

I shook my head. "Okay, now I see."

This was one of those Perry Mason–type attorneys; maybe God would move through her.

I really wanted to get my glasses. The detectives were holding them as evidence because the witness had described me as wearing thick glasses. That was exactly why I needed them. I could hardly see beyond my nose without those glasses! The prosecutors refused to give them up. My attorney made a request at every court appearance, but the judge consistently ruled against it once the prosecutor stated his opposition. My uncle, who had a similar prescription, let me borrow a pair of his once he could get them to me. I went nearly three months without those glasses, causing me headaches beyond imagination, but I was an inmate, and no one really wanted to hear my problems.

Evil does not respect good and good does not respect evil.

Speaking of the prosecutor, I later learned a bit about his feelings toward me. He wrote in his report to the judge that although I was a college graduate, I had graduated with a low GPA. When I later read this I wanted to go to his office and shout my feelings about whether he could have even completed the curriculum at Drexel University, one of the toughest academic schools on the East Coast. He also mentioned that I was hired by the IRS during a period when the federal government wanted to hire more minorities. According to him, I was hired simply because I was black. What really surprised me is that he didn't mince words when he made these statements. After reading that part and a few other choice sections of his report, I wanted to go to his office and punch him. Even now, after nearly thirty years, as I write this, punching him out seems like a good option, but that would be criminal.

I eventually lost my case. There were few meetings between my attorney and the prosecutor. At first my attorney said I could be looking at thirteen years max: eight for the armed robbery and five for the attempted robbery. Both charges carried two-year enhancements for doing a crime with a weapon.

During the plea bargaining, my main hope was that they would drop the gun charge. It was a pellet gun, for God's sake. My attorney argued that point, but to no avail.

I tried to get someone to go to the spot where I tossed the "gun," but no one seemed to care to do that. If they actually thought it was a real gun, loaded and all, it would seem to me that the officers would at least go look. Couldn't this lead to a dangerous situation, a loaded gun lying in the brush of a freeway off-ramp? This would seem true especially since they never found a gun in the car and the people at the liquor store said I had a gun. Why wouldn't they follow the only lead they had?

I truly believe that they did, in fact, follow the lead that I gave them. Either they got there and there was no gun or they got there, found the pellet gun, and didn't report it, as it would hamper their gun charge. However, the prosecutor never suggested one way or another what happened to the "gun."

THINGS CAN ALWAYS GET WORSE

WHEN I GOT back to the dorm, I was in for another surprise. I was pulled out of the infirmary and told by the officer of the day that I was being transferred to J Tank. Oh my God! J Tank was the home of the Gladiators. Didn't hardly a night go by without us hearing "man down in J Tank." What did I do to deserve this?

I gathered my little canteen bag together, rolled up my sheets and blanket, and followed the officer out into the main jail. I said my goodbyes quickly, but I'm sure everyone could tell that I was having major concerns. As I had learned to do during my frequent trips to the hospital for various procedures, I began saying the Twenty-third Psalm. My lips moved, but the words were in my head.

When we got to the entry of the notorious cell block, one deputy passed me over to the next one. Surprisingly, I was able to find a top bunk about halfway down the dorm. As was my custom, I put my canteen bag with my toiletries, snacks, and cigarettes under my mattress. A young Mexican slept on the lower bunk. I don't think five minutes passed before I heard some rustling and felt the bag being tugged from underneath my bed. I quickly looked over the side of the bed and there he was, my new bunkie, going through my bag.

He stared at me. The moment of truth.

I stared back. "What the hell do you think you're doing?" I said, snatching my bag back.

I did not hesitate. If nothing else I had learned in the prison system that he who hesitates has already lost. My bunkie laid back down and that was it. I still knew my stuff wasn't safe. I surveyed the dorm. There seemed to be two shot callers. One was Mexican and the other was black. The noise was maddening. It was like being on the bus or in one of the holding tanks, only louder. So much so, it was hard to make out any one conversation.

"Really, Lord? Is this really where I have to be? I'm too old for this."

Why didn't you think of that before you started robbing liquor stores?

My inner voice continued the conversation, interspersed with prayerful *why mes* and *help me Jesuses* throughout.

When it was time to go to chow, everyone begin making their way to the gate. I saw quite a few blacks giving their canteen to the black I later found out was called Boss Man. When I walked past him, I threw my bag onto his bunk and said a quick "You got me?"

I was relieved to hear him say, "Sure do, bro."

Another trip to the dining room. This time I wasn't caught by surprise. I was quiet and ate just as fast as the next man. I don't think they gave us any more than ten minutes to eat, but most folks learned to get it all down in that amount of time. There was no chatter, only the sounds of eating and the occasional "salt," "juice" as requests were kept to a minimum. When we were finished—or, should I say, when time was up—we jumped up, lined up, and made our way out of the dining room.

Back to J Tank.

The night was just beginning. I had heard the stories, sometimes even seeing the results when they brought the loser of a fight down to the infirmary.

I didn't even venture to do anything other than grab my bag from Boss Man with a quick thanks as I saw others doing.

Soon it was time for the med line. They called out names and by now, with all I had going on, I received at least two or three pills for sleep and anxiety. In the infirmary, I had agreements with other inmates and would barter for their meds. This helped me sleep most of the day and throughout the night. As we all know, time flies when you're having fun or asleep, and fun wasn't an option for me.

My name was called, and I quickly made my way to the gate, bag in hand. The nurse checked my ID bracelet, even though I'm sure he recognized me. I got my meds and got back in bed.

One thing I soon found out was that the lights are never turned off in the main jail. In the infirmary, the lights stayed on too, but they were dimmed to a reasonable degree of dusk.

Not here. The lights stayed on bright throughout the night. I didn't plan on waiting to see if they ever got dimmer, though. I took my meds and waited for sleep to rescue me from the asylum.

As I began to doze off, I noticed many of the young Mexicans shadow boxing. I had long ago learned to sleep with my shoes on, especially if I had gotten wind of something going down. In this dorm, just to keep your shoes would probably entail keeping them on. Even then, I'm sure some guys got them taken.

The dorm had somewhat quieted down. The quiet before the storm, as some say.

Before I could fall off to sleep, I noticed a space had been cleared toward the rear of the dorm. The gates to the cell block would soon be blocked by inmates who would provide cover, so deputies couldn't get a clear view of what was going on.

Suddenly the first pair of gladiators began boxing. There were loud shouts as homeboys called out encouragement to the men fighting. All the fights were brown on brown. To throw blacks into the fray would quickly escalate into a riot.

When someone got beaten to a pulp or just gave up, which didn't happen, often the next pair of mixed arts fighters—I use the term loosely—began their bout. I dozed off, but was awakened throughout the night as the fighting continued. I'm sure it ended at some desig-nated time, but all I can say is when I woke to get ready for breakfast, it was over. The lights never went out.

The next day, on the way back from the dining room, God smiled and I laughed on the inside. One of the deputies noticed me as I was making my way back to my new residence. He pulled me aside and called to one of his buddies. He could not believe that someone would have sent me out into the main population with a piece of metal on my hand. The splint that held one of my fingers straight outside the cast was made of metal. He quickly called out to a sergeant, pointing out the metal splint.

The sergeant gave him one of those disbelieving looks and told him to take me up to J Tank and let me get my stuff and get my behind back to the infirmary. As I packed up my few little belongings, I became very popular. Friends and homies came out of the woodwork as they asked me to leave them my change, toiletries, and snacks.

"I still need them," I said. "I'm not being released, just moved back to the infirmary."

Back in the infirmary, Geronimo smiled. "I saved your bunk for you."

I greeted the rest of the guys and took my usual position.

A DAY OF RECKONING

S OON I WAS back in court for sentencing. I expected to meet with
my attorney, but she was somewhere on another case. How could
she do this to me? I needed her to argue my request to speak to
the judge in his chambers. I needed her to argue the fact that the so-
called gun was not a gun at all and could not be considered as such.
I needed her, because we had built a relationship and I trusted her to
fight for me.

It was not to be.

The lady who represented me was the same one Geronimo had.
He called her a "dump truck," meaning her clients got dumped fairly
quickly. Served up on a platter to the prosecutor to do as he wished.

This is the problem with having to use public defenders. They're
not on your payroll, they're paid by the county. They seem to be there
only to ensure that the system gives a resemblance of fairness. I'm
in no way saying they all act unfairly. I am sure that many are very
committed attorneys, but some are not and, just as in other careers,
they seem to be there just for a paycheck.

It's easier to fall into this category when you work for the government, because the government has your back. You're going to receive
a paycheck regardless. It's not like you have to advertise or display
your victories versus defeats. You're a county employee, the same

as the prosecutor and the judge. Many times they go out to lunch together and attend the same Christmas parties.

Perhaps it's the situations they find themselves in. Many times they are assigned cases only moments before appearing in court, as was the case on this day. It's just a bummer for the defendant, me in this instance, when one of the biggest decisions made by the court is being brought before a defender who has no knowledge of the case.

One of the other inmates being sentenced that day was named Tracy. We had been in the infirmary together on two occasions. When Tracy was first arrested it was for the same charge I faced: armed robbery. Tracy was very young, early twenties at best. He was also blond. Somehow, Tracy was released. I assumed his parents paid his bail.

However, in about a month's time, Tracy was back. Incredibly, it was for a second armed robbery. This time there was no bail. Tracy was sentenced first and received four years: two for the robberies and two for the gun.

Soon it was my turn. Although my attorney did mention my request to speak with the judge in closed chambers, he saw no reason to do that. "If you have anything to say, you can say it in open court."

Naturally, I wasn't going to bring up my background in open court. Word would reach the jail before I did. "No thank you, Your Honor."

The judge sentenced me to serve five years in the state penitentiary: three for the robbery and two for the gun. That was it. I felt a calm come over me.

Only later did the devil speak to me about the injustice he wanted me to dwell on. *How did Tracy, who had two armed robberies, get less time than me?* my inner voice would ask.

Even the bus ride back didn't seem as bad. When I got back into the infirmary, I told the fellas what had happened. I began to be treated with a little more respect. It wasn't so much the amount of time that I received that gained their admiration. The move from being designated a "county inmate" to a "state convict" was almost looked at as a promotion. I had crossed a line. I was now a convicted felon, a title that would stick with me for life (unfortunately)—a title honored by other convicts, but dishonored by society in general. The guys said I probably had a week, maybe two, before I "caught the chain": prison vernacular for my trip to the next destination, California's massive state prison system.

I called my mom and told her. She wanted to bring the kids to visit before I left. I told her that wasn't necessary. I could get visits once I went into the state prison system. For what I believe was the first time since this began, I told my mother I was sorry for all the pain I had put her through over the last few years. I told her, and meant it sincerely, that God would work this out. The next time I would talk to her would be from the state prison in Chino, not far at all from where she lived.

That week went by very quickly. The bus to prison left on Thursdays, and on the following Thursday my name was called. I woke Geronimo and gave him all the dimes I had. We weren't best friends or nothing, but we had built an acquaintance and I appreciated him for who he was. I had already said my goodbyes to the other long-termers the night before. I made my way to the holding cell for state prisoners.

The ride was not bad at all. I felt free.

STATESIDE

THE JOURNEY TO the state prison in Chino was calm, almost somber, compared to the joy rides back and forth to court. The only thing of note happened when someone spotted a dead dairy cow and shouted, "That's probably tonight's dinner!"

We all chuckled. Chino was a town known for dairies, and there were dairy farms throughout the rural areas.

When we got to the central jail we pulled into the sally port. The underside of the bus was searched via mirror, and our papers were presented by the county deputy to the state correctional officer.

The gun towers were very evident. The prison at Chino had three yards. One was Chino Central, where we were going now. It was a high-security yard, used primarily for parole violators or high-profile prisoners on their way to other sites. The other was Chino West, a reception center for lower-level inmates entering the prison system from southern California. The third was CIM—Chino Institute for Men—a minimum-security yard for inmates who were very low security risks. Most inmates and convicts were eventually taken to Chino West, where they were evaluated before being sent to one of the many prisons throughout the state. All first-timers and those who had caught new cases were taken to Central first for their initial processing.

After the bus parked in front of a nondescript building, we were herded off and barked at along the way until we got inside. It reminded me of movies I had seen about Army recruits. Once inside, a drill sergeant–type correctional officer, or CO, yelled for us to remove all of our clothes and dispose of any unnecessary belongings. Everything said by the CO seemed to be five or ten decibels above normal conversation level.

I quickly got out of my orange jump suit. Good riddance to that thing. The only other thing I had was my California ID. For some reason, I tore it up and followed everyone else into the shower. We showered and sprayed down for lice.

Don't they know black folks don't have lice? my inner voice smirked.

Once we came out we were given the new uniform: a pair of underwear, grey socks, blue jeans, a blue button-down shirt and hard-soled brown lace-up shoes. We were marched into another room and told to give a urine specimen.

I was so anxious I couldn't pee, no matter how hard I tried. Finally, I was able to get an acceptable amount into the bottle. We were marched into another room and assigned to cells.

To chants of "fish" by convicts already there, we were marched up the stairs and into the cell blocks. I and another black were assigned to the same cell. He took the top bunk and I gladly took the bottom because of the cast. This cast had been on my hand for nearly four months, but I was used to it by this time. The cell door was shut, and me and my cellie did our best to get to know each other.

I wasn't as open at sharing as I had been when I was first arrested. I did tell him that this was my first prison term.

He shared that he had been here before. He gave me a few pointers that he felt would help me. We talked about family stuff and where we were from.

When it was time to eat, our cell door slid open, and we made our way along the tier and downstairs to the dining room with the rest of the guys. The food here proved to be hot and a lot better quality. You could eat wherever you chose, but I noticed quickly that all the blacks were in one corner of the room. The whites and Mexicans were interspersed throughout, but it appeared the races stuck to the same tables. This would be a trend throughout every state prison concerning every activity where you actually had a choice, from eating to weight lifting, the blacks stayed segregated. However, there was still segregation amid the segregation. The Crips, Bloods and Pirus were pocketed together whenever possible.

We were back in our cells in no time. Once nighttime came, an amazing thing happened. The lights went out. It wasn't pitch black, but pretty darn close. It was as much darkness as I had experienced since leaving the hospital.

There's a Whodini song that says "the freaks come out at night." Here it was no different. Yelling and obscene comments rang throughout the cell block.

The guys who had been there a while naturally had friends and acquaintances. If someone was in a cell with a new inmate, they had to let everyone know, especially if the guy looked afraid or effeminate, or, God forbid, started to cry. If this happened, the seasoned inmate let everyone know what his cellie could expect later that night.

Later, when it came time for the first count, it just happened to be a black female correctional officer doing the counting on our tier. She didn't seem to mind the comments concerning her anatomy. In fact, she gave back as good as she took, which only served to intensify the lewd comments.

It was easy to fall asleep in the darkness I had missed for so long. I was awakened early the next morning by the sound of my name being called among others. My cellie told me I would probably be transferred to Chino West, the reception center. Because he was a parole violator, he would either complete his time here or be moved to the prison he had paroled from. After breakfast, we said our goodbyes and I was on the short ride to Chino West.

The West yard held about eight or ten trailers, each large enough to house a dorm full of men, with restrooms and showers. There were no bars, but the gun towers reminded you that there were indeed boundaries.

I was assigned a bunk in the Mariposa Dorm. There was not much to do, but I soon made the acquaintance of three or four brothers and we hung out together. One happened to be from Pomona and knew one of my female cousins who had grown up across the street from where I stayed with my mom. To say that he was infatuated with her would be an understatement.

We ate our meals together, played dominoes, and began solving the problems of the world. Naturally, we were asked, "What did you do?" I told them about my drug addiction and my armed robbery crimes. A couple of the guys thought my using a pellet gun landed part way between funny and crazy and was an example of what drug use could lead to.

I don't remember that any of us had been in prison before, but being locked up wasn't new to everyone. These guys were all a lot younger than I, but I've always been blessed to look younger than I actually am. All my newfound friends were there due to drug-related crimes. None of them were very well educated. In fact, as time passed, I became the official letter writer for most of them.

We had to clear the dorms after chow in the morning and again after lunch in the afternoon. We had to have a medical excuse to stay on our beds. So most of our time was spent outside, regardless of the weather, unless there was a severe storm.

As time went on, I got accustomed to my new surroundings. I don't remember there being a canteen or whether or not we could receive packages from home. The planned time to be spent there was so short, packages wouldn't have made sense.

There were inmates there who were actually doing their time. They stayed in a separate dorm and worked in various positions within the facility. These guys were part of the prison work crew, called PWCs. They made up the kitchen crew, the visitors' room monitors, landscapers, clerks, and other necessary roles.

I thought this would be the place for me. There were very few arguments, and I don't recall any fights. This could have been due to the fact that we were all there for the long haul. No one was coming in to do weekends or leaving one day and showing up the next after being re-arrested. There was a permanency to being in prison. If you stabbed someone today, there was nowhere to hide, so you'd better watch your back for the duration because you could be the one getting shanked tomorrow.

One day I was called to the administration building to meet with my counselor and begin the process of determining my first housing assignment within California's massive prison system. I was given what I believe to be an IQ test, then sent to a waiting room.

While I waited, an old acquaintance walked by. He was an employee. He did a double take as he saw me sitting there.

I looked at him and smiled. "Yeah, Amos, it's me."

Amos was a close friend of the lady who lived next door to my mom. Her parents had moved out and given her the house. Once she got strung out on cocaine, it sort of became a crack house.

It started as a place where just a few of us would go to get high. Later, she and her husband began to let gang-banging youngsters take over the house on the first and fifteenth, when money was plentiful due to the government checks that came out on those days. These kids would drive up in Mercedeses, BMWs, and all sorts of luxury cars. They paid my neighbors in cocaine and turned the house into a full-fledged crack house. There was so much traffic in and out, it's surprising it never got shut down. I'm sure other neighbors knew, because my uncle talked about what a disgrace it was.

I first met Amos before the house had become so popular. He got paid once a month. He could be counted on to come on a Friday and stay until Monday. We began to depend on him coming by, because he kind of kept the house going. In the beginning he was the man, giving everyone a freebie.

However, as the first day passed and we moved into the second and third, he was still chasing that first hit, and no way was he going to catch it. Guys like him would get mad at everybody there when they realized that their money was gone and they had this terrible jones or withdrawal symptoms. He, like me, had become a casualty of the war against drugs. When he was broke he was broke for the rest of the month.

Amos stared at me for a few minutes longer and then quickly walked by.

I watched him as he left, knowing I would be the topic of conversation the next time he was at the crack house. Now I knew where he worked, but that's where it ended.

I never saw him again.

When I finally got to the counselor's office, he went over my background. He mentioned the violence of my crime. He asked about my family ties. I told him about my mom, uncles, and kids. This was when I began to understand how the California Department of Corrections, the CDC, calculated its point system. This system told them what level of penitentiary you would go to. It was based on a number of things, most importantly the type of crime. Other indicators included family ties, criminal history, disciplinary actions while in custody, degree of flight risk and more. Your score could take you from a level one, minimum-security, to a level five, high-security prison.

When the counselor finished tallying my score, I was at a twenty-six, which put me in the medium-security level.

"Do you have any preferences as to where you want to go?" he asked.

"I'd really prefer to stay here as a PWC."

"Is that a good idea? So many guys are processed through this site. What if one of them recognizes you from your law enforcement days?"

"That's unlikely, because most of the crimes I investigated were white collar. But I have to admit, there is a possibility." I added California Rehabilitation Center in Norco and California Men's Colony in San Luis Obispo. Norco was the closest, and my chief concern was getting visits from mom and the kids.

SMALL TALK

WHEN WE WERE outdoors, most of us sat on the bleachers and talked about women or past and future crimes.

One day I ran into a group of guys from Pomona. Even though I had spent the last year and a half before my arrest getting loaded, I never really made friends. The kids' mom did, however, and these guys recognized me because of her.

Earthy was one of the guys I did remember. Pam had convinced me to give him a ride somewhere. I recalled the strong odor of "sherm," or PCP, that he was carrying in a mayonnaise jar when he got in my car. My guess was that he was taking it somewhere to dip cigarettes into it and make sherm sticks, which had become so popular among those we called the shermheads of Pomona.

He told the other guys who my wife was. They immediately began to describe her to a T.

Before one guy could describe her in more ways than Earthy felt I should have known, he quieted them. "Watch it now, she was his wife..."

I also ran into a Mexican that I had met in the county jail. His name was Chato. I mention Chato for two reasons. First, he came up to me on the yard and asked how I was doing. This in itself was unusual because, as Gene had told me months ago, blacks and Mexicans don't mix in the pen. Second, Chato broke out what had to be one of the skinniest joints that I had ever seen. As we walked, he told me to light it up. Wanting to still be considered "down for mine," I did as asked.

I took a couple of quick hits and passed it back to him.

He did the same. We shared until it was gone.

I must admit I got a slight buzz—the last marijuana buzz I've ever had.

I wonder how much additional time that could have cost me if we had gotten busted.

DAD

WHILE AT CHINO West, I got a surprise visit. My mom came, but with her was my dad. I haven't mentioned much about him, because we didn't have all that great of a relationship. He was proud when I followed in his footsteps by playing football and earning a college scholarship. However, he was really let down when I quit to begin my family.

To say the least, I was surprised to see him. He was a retired police officer, former homicide detective with the Cleveland PD. At the time of his visit, he had been working for several years as a bodyguard for Don King, the fight promoter. So I guess you could say he had seen his share of criminals, not just behind bars. Naturally, too, it makes a whole lot of difference when it's your son.

Just a few years earlier, he had visited my office at the IRS. Again, there were signs of pride. He was in law enforcement, and at the time, so was I. He did feel a need to let me know not to mention my employment to Don King.

I let him down again when I lost my job. But that was over now. I said, "Dad my near death experience was a real wake up call for me. I think before this I always questioned the existence of God. Now I know. He saved my life! I don't know why but God showed me He has a purpose for me. I don't know what purpose I have, but I must be special."

I don't really remember how my dad responded. That alone lets me know that he wasn't too excited. Up until several years ago he was not what I call a religious man and like other visitors, he did not respond much to my newfound salvation or my testimony. It would be a few years before I saw him again.

LIFE REVIEW

- In your life today, do you seem to have more blessings and peace or trouble and fighting? Explain.

- Who are your five closest friends/relatives?

- Are they helping you to make good choices that will bring favor or bad choices that will bring trouble?

- God wants to be your closest friend. He can help you out of your trouble and bring you peace. You just need to ask Him and keep asking Him. You can start right now. Just ask Him.

2 PART TWO
LIFE INSIDE

FOR THE LORD HEARETH THE POOR, AND DESPISETH NOT HIS PRISONERS.
— PSALM 69:33

CALIFORNIA REHABILITATION CENTER

ONE OF THE guys in my circle came to tell me our names were finally on the assignment list. We would be going to the California Rehabilitation Center, or CRC, in Norco.

Besides Chino, this was actually at the top of my list. I didn't know much about it, other than it was only a few miles away from Chino. I would still be within easy driving distance for my mom, who did not drive the freeways of California.

Norco is a small rural area about forty miles east of Los Angeles, about fifteen miles from Pomona. The bus ride from Chino took about twenty minutes.

The process of checking in at CRC was rather simple. There wasn't any.

We were assigned to the Hotel, a tall white building that had been converted from a hotel to a twelve-story dormitory. We were assigned to the twelfth floor which, from the looks of it, had never been used. The bedding and linen seemed fresh—we could have been at the Mission Inn in Riverside.

My bunkie was a Crip who called himself Trey Dog. His first name was Tracy. Neither of us had been to the penitentiary before, but he seemed better suited for it. Trey had many stories to tell, all criminal. He appeared to be about twenty-two or twenty-three years of age, from Grape Street in Watts, known for its gang activity.

For obvious reasons, I didn't have much to share. I had children who were nearly his age. In fact, the first letter I wrote home to my oldest son highlighted the life of Trey.

My oldest son, Rasheed, was by now well on his way to a life of crime. I had heard from my mom that he was spending more time at a neighbor's house than at home. This particular neighbor was not the role model you wanted for your child. Although the man had children himself, he was believed to be a drug dealer. My mom and uncle felt he was using Rasheed to sell drugs, a common practice then, because youngsters like him would get very little time, if any, when caught.

He pampered Rasheed by giving him his own off-road vehicle, a dirt bike meant to be ridden in the countryside. Rasheed rode it throughout Pomona, and before he was even old enough to drive, he had accumulated numerous tickets.

The letter that I wrote to him reflected Trey Dog's plight. I guess I was making an effort to scare Rasheed straight; but in hindsight, I may have glorified the life of a gangster if anything. At that moment, I realized how the only glorification I want to promote from now on is that given to Jesus Christ, my Lord and Savior, and so I began looking for more ways to consciously do that.

Life in the Hotel was fairly uneventful. It was not connected to the main units of CRC, so we kind of felt isolated from everyone else. I believe that CRC used to be some sort of military base before the Department of Corrections took it over. As I noted earlier, CRC was a medium-security yard. It generally took the medium-security inmates that overflowed from the regular prison system, since it was initially set up as a drug rehabilitation center. The Hotel had its own yard and dining room. It was being used at the time as sort of a reception center to house inmates before they went to the "bottoms," the inmate word for the rest of the complex.

Besides the Hotel there were four other units. They were simply numbered two through five. The really unusual thing about CRC was that one of the units, Unit Four, housed women. Each unit consisted of portable housing, similar to large trailers. These were the dorms.

The dining room was in the middle of the bottoms and fed each of the dorms. The women's dorms sat atop a steep hill, overlooking the remainder of the facility. In addition to the women's dorms, several administrative offices sat up on the hill as well. The men's visiting room, the chapel, the warehouses, and the infirmary were all within the confines of the men's unit. The women had a similar setup in their area.

Classes were offered to the inmates. Some of these had waiting lists, depending on their popularity, for example auto mechanics. There was also a large track and several weight lifting areas throughout the complex and a gym.

CRC Norco also housed what the system called "N-Numbers." These were people who had caught nonviolent drug-related cases. If they qualified for the program, when they completed, they would leave without a criminal record. It would be as if they had been in a sanitarium or something. The great thing about the N-Number was that they could be released in as little as six months. However, they carried a lengthy parole period, seven years, and many inmates refused this designation because of this. I had heard about the program when I was in the county jail. Naturally, I was told that I wouldn't qualify due to the violent nature of my crime. Yet here I was, at CRC. However, I had a regular CDC number, D-22855.

Why me? Because you said so, Lord!

HOME SWEET HOME

INALLY THE DAY came when my name appeared on the movement sheet. I was being transferred to Dorm 50 in Unit Five. As I made my way toward my new home, I got a chance to see most of the complex. It was huge. Dorm 50 was naturally just before Dorm 51, which I had heard through the grapevine was designated the "old man's dorm."

When I first got to CRC this was pretty much an open shot, from one end of the complex to the other. However, as California's prisons began to fill due to overcrowding, CRC became more of a Level 2–3 yard than a straight Level 2.

With this change came many more.

Additional gun towers and search lights went up, compared with the one or two that were there when we first arrived. There was also more security between units as gates went up and officer-patrolled checkpoints were at the entry to each unit. This would all happen sometime in 1987, but for now, things were pretty serene.

When I got to Dorm 50, I checked in with the correction officer. He assigned me to a bottom bunk. When I got there, I found out that my assignment hadn't gone over well with the other inmates. Bottom bunks were given out according to seniority, but my cast-bound hand allowed me to override that process.

The dorm was loud, but not extremely so. There was a large TV room as you first walked in, adjacent to the CO's office. A pay phone hung on the wall outside the office. I didn't spend a lot of time in the TV room, but I later found out that each day was assigned to a race. These days rotated. So if the blacks had control of the TV on Mondays, the Mexicans would have control on Tuesdays and the whites on Wednesdays and so on.

Because people were there for longer periods of time, there seemed to be more camaraderie. If World Cup Soccer was on, there might be allowances made by the other races to allow the Mexicans to watch that. The same with other cultural types of shows. The Mexicans seemed to have the upper hand. First, there were more of them, and second, they pretty much stuck together.

The blacks, on the other hand, had a problem because of the gang situation. The Crips, Bloods, and other spin-off groups kept the blacks separated within their own race. On rare occasions, the blacks would recognize their quandary and the gangs would call a truce. An example would be a brown on black dispute that could put all blacks at risk.

As far as the whites went, there just weren't enough of them at Norco, so they tended to side with the Mexicans. The language difference was a natural barrier. There were times when Mexicans put on shows that were in Spanish, and the rest of the dorm just had to deal with it.

Surprisingly, most of the inmates loved to watch the soap operas, so these were on throughout the week.

There was an older gentleman in the bunk next to mine. He introduced himself as King. I soon found out that we were both Christians. King seemed elated and so was I.

He was a very good artist and made money on the side selling authentic greeting cards, but he also painted on canvas using photos he found in the National Geographic magazines he collected. He showed me some of his artwork, and it was fantastic.

Over the years I spent in the pen, it never ceased to amaze me just how much talent there was within the inmates, much of it artwork.

King and I spent most of our waking hours together. On the nights that the Protestants led chapel, we went to church together. There I met many other Christian brothers—black, white, and brown—who had given their lives over to the Lord. Some sincerely, and some not so much.

King had transferred to CRC from Soledad State Prison. His crime revolved around drinking, but it went a little further than that.

King and his wife had a few drinks and started jostling around in their second-story apartment. King pushed her, and she somehow fell out of the window. King ran downstairs to help her. When he arrived she appeared unconscious. He began to nudge her with his foot, trying to revive her. "I started to kick her a little harder, thinking maybe she was just playing. Before I knew it, I was angry with her for embarrassing me in front of all the people who had begun to gather around. I kicked harder and used a few choice words, thinking that that would bring her to her senses." King was immediately carted off to jail. His wife was taken to the hospital.

I'm not sure how her testimony went, but I do know she ended up in a wheelchair with paralysis in her lower extremities.

King ended up with a long sentence to state prison.

Besides going to the chapel to hear the preaching, teaching, praise, and worship, our favorite pastime became checkers and gin rummy. No matter how hard I tried, I could not win a game of checkers to save my life. Likewise, I beat King pretty regularly in gin rummy.

Besides talking about the Bible, we spent our separate quiet time painting (King) and writing and doing Bible studies (me).

Soon a third party joined our group. I called him Mr. Smith. I always included the "Mr." when I addressed him because he was much older than me. While King was in his forties, Mr. Smith was in his sixties. He didn't have much time for games, but he loved to talk about the Word of God. He had a Dake Bible and swore by its commentaries. We took turns teaching Bible studies on the picnic table outside our dorm.

I learned more about God in prison than I ever did before. Mr. Smith also happened to work at the chapel as a janitor. He was very familiar with the prison chaplain. He also knew all the Protestant inmate staff who were clerks. Mr. Smith had come down from Folsom. He told me the story of when the bus first pulled up to the gates outside Folsom. He said there was a cemetery outside the gates and a large sign you couldn't miss that read **Folsom State Prison,**

LEAVE ALL DREAMS BEHIND

Mr. Smith could always get a laugh out of us when he told us about the first gunshots he heard while on the tier. "When the shooting was done and everyone was cleared to open their cell doors, a cry went up about the dead brother in the upper bunk of cell 15. I wasn't dead, Smith said, but as close to being scared to death as you can get. I was frozen to my mattress. When the C.O's came down and checked me out, they cracked up laughing when his first words were; 'y'all gotta get me up outta here. I'm too old for this kind of stuff.'" Smith became known as "dead man walkin" for a short period while at Folsom.

CHOW TIME

WHENEVER POSSIBLE, WE ate our meals together. Mr. Smith was in Unit Three, so our dorms were called at separate times. However, once you got into the dining room, there was no one hammering down on the table telling you to leave and, unlike the County Jail, you had some time to sit and wait for your homies. However, there were times when we were on lockdown and the security was so tight this couldn't be done. During these times, prisoners were fed one or two dorms at a time, and eating time was limited.

The cafeterias at CRC had tables similar to those on the outside. They would usually seat six to eight inmates. As mentioned earlier, blacks kept to themselves in one corner of the room. As time went on, I met many other brothers. Usually they were Christian, and we all sat together and talked about the Word. We didn't talk much about home, unless it was something extraordinary. We shared our release dates and all looked forward to walking out of the prison gates.

The chow hall was a place for social gathering. At our table, which was usually made up of the guys who frequented the chapel, the talk usually revolved around the Lord. We discussed various Scriptures or revelations God had given us. We also talked about upcoming events or the weekly services. This was especially true when the prison became more security-conscious and the units were kept separate from each other. If the guys you knew weren't on your unit or in your dorm, you might not see them until the next church service.

CRC meals are pretty predictable, especially breakfasts. We all knew that on Sunday mornings we got real eggs, sunny side up or over easy. On Thursdays, we were guaranteed to get sweet rolls. I think the sweet rolls were number one on the popularity list. A sweet roll could easily fetch a pack of cigarettes back at the dorm.

Thursdays just happened to be my fast day. I fasted every Thursday from midnight until 4 p.m. I have found over the years that there is nothing more rewarding than a spiritual fast. Up until about a year ago, my Thursday fasts were consistent. Just like I didn't let the Thursday morning sweet rolls get to me in prison, I haven't let numerous other temptations get to me on the outside that would cause me to skip my fast day. I'm not saying I've never missed a fast day, but I will say that missing a fast day, particularly while incarcerated, was a rarity.

BOOKER SAYS . . .

Spiritual fasting requires self-discipline and self-sacrifice. So why do I do it? Because it tells God, "I'm serious about wanting to get close to You. I really need an answer to my prayer and this is what I'm willing to give up on my part to get it." Or "God, you said that these types of demons are only defeated through fasting and prayer. I need victory in this battle." God rewards a person who is dedicated to Him in body as well as heart and soul.

The chow line always seemed to be unfair to me, even though when you went through the cafeteria-style line you couldn't see the server, and they couldn't see you. I always seemed to get short-changed. No matter what was on the menu, my pork chop or chicken leg always seemed to be smaller than that of the guy ahead of me or behind me. The guy in front of me would get a piece of meat that would nearly tilt the plate. My mouth would start watering, just looking at it, but when it came my turn, my portion would be so small it was almost unidentifiable.

As time went on and I came to know the guys in the dorm who worked in the kitchen, I would pay a pack of smokes to get a decent-size portion to eat at my bunk. It actually got to be comical. Chilly, my main food connection, would automatically bring me something back when his shift was over. We'd have a good laugh. He'd have cigarettes and I'd have a decent chop and be happy as a fat rat in a cheese factory.

BOOKER SAYS . . .

We can't do life alone. We all need connections, but any connection is only as good as the amount of respect I give them. Give and take equally. Win-Win. These are the rules of a fruitful connection. My connections didn't influence me into their way of thinking and behaving because I now lived for the friendship of Jesus. But maybe I influenced them just by being different.

What connections have you made?

Are they influencing you or are you influencing them? In what way?

Occasionally, there would be a CRC Special, where if I had the money on the books, I could order KFC or Dunkin' Donuts. These days would only come around about once every three to four months.

There were many times, besides fast days, that I just wouldn't go to the chow hall. As I was able to build up my own personal canteen, I'd break out some tuna, mayonnaise, and a cup of noodles and make a good ole "spread." Spreads were something that were apparently popular throughout the California Department of Corrections system. Sometimes four, five, or even ten guys might get together and have their own spread. What you put in it was usually up to you, but they always contained at the very least noodles, mayonnaise, and a canned meat. A seafood spread would contain tuna, oysters, or clams. Sometimes we would get an onion, bell pepper, hot peppers, or salsa, and they would all become part of the spread. Some guys became famous for their spreads.

My wife and I, to this day, still occasionally break out the fixins and prepare a good old-fashioned spread. The kids used to laugh when we told them the origins of our recipes.

OLD BUSINESS

IN THE SPRING of 1986, my cast was finally removed. I went to sick call, which was always at five or six o'clock in the morning. I think they wanted to make sure you were seriously sick and not just wanting to go there and hang out.

The process required letting the dorm CO know, and he would make sure I was wakened in the morning and given a pass.

Once I got to see one of the nurses, all I had to mention was the fact that the cast had been on for about eight months.

"Oh, my God," she said. "I hope you still have an arm under there."

Soon my name appeared on the movement list. I waited for my name to be called that day and went to Receiving and Release—what we called R&R—to catch my ride to the hospital. This was the first time I had been out in the real world since arriving at CRC.

The drive to the hospital was uneventful, although it brought with it a sore reminder of how it felt to be cuffed and shackled. The people we met in the hallways, who instinctively gave us a lot of room, brought back memories of the county jail. I had almost forgotten I wasn't a free man. I was really accustomed to my situation.

The cast was removed, and my left hand and arm looked horrible. They were ten shades lighter than the rest of my body and about half the size of their right counterparts.

I had submitted a form to the federal court requesting to be taken back for sentencing on my parole violation. Not long after the cast was removed, my name appeared on the movement list again.

I went back to R&R the following day and was picked up by two US marshals. There was one other passenger, a young black man being taken back for sentencing regarding an arson case.

On the way to Los Angeles, we also picked up a young black woman from a halfway house. She was being returned to a federal prison for rules violations.

When we arrived at the courthouse, it brought back old memories, as I recalled the better side of processing. What seemed like years ago, it was me taking the fingerprints and getting the inmate ready for photos. Now I was on the other side.

We were finger printed and photos were taken. The two of us guys were placed in a holding cell waiting for transportation to the federal penitentiary at Terminal Island. Once the court attendees came back from their day in court, we were all escorted to the bus.

The bus ride was remarkable only because the person I sat next to had been arrested for numerous bank robberies. He was a young white man, and he told me that on the day he was captured he had robbed four banks on the same day. He talked about the sensation of running his hands through the piles of money on the passenger seat next to him as he drove from bank to bank. Although he didn't use a gun, he was looking at much more time than I had received. The FBI, prosecutors, and judge just did not play when it came to bank robbery.

My arson friend and I ended up in the same cell at Terminal Island, which is on an island near San Pedro, about thirty miles south of Los Angeles. It's close to shore, and a short trip across a bridge got you there. We were assigned to a sort of high-power building. Our movement was very much restricted. Meals were brought to our cells and delivered through slots in the cell doors. If we wanted to use the phone, it was given to us the same way.

When it was time to use the shower, we were cuffed through the door and taken to a shower cell. Once we were inside, the door was closed and our cuffs removed through the slot in the door. In the TV room, the procedure was the same. Just me and him, cuffed and taken to the TV room and then locked in there.

We had no contact with other inmates besides a trustee who came by periodically. Our outside activity consisted of being taken to a fenced yard with a basketball hoop and a basketball that was deflated. That was some irony.

The trustee was an older black gentleman. I didn't recognize him, but when he said his name, I was surprised. He had once been one of the biggest dope dealers in Southern California.

The memory came back immediately. Working on a short under-cover assignment, I and another agent had gone to the gentleman's wedding reception at the Ambassador Hotel on Wilshire Boulevard.

The agent and I spent most of our time outside the hotel collecting license plate numbers from the Bentleys, Rolls-Royces, and other super luxury cars that graced the parking lot. We talked our way inside and even danced and ate a few of the appetizers. My partner got an opportunity to kiss the bride on the cheek.

Now, this was several years later, and I was the furthest thing from the trustee's mind. He even brought me a pack of cigarettes, which I accepted, although I had recently quit. They could come in handy later.

When it was time for my court appearance, I was a little appre-hensive. What if the judge decided to throw the book at me? The bus ride to Los Angeles seemed long, probably due to traffic. I was cuffed and escorted from the lockup to the same courtroom where the same judge had so generously given me two years probation for my crime against the government.

Lo and behold, I ran into another memory on my way up to the court. One of the IRS agents I used to work with got on the ele-vator on the lobby floor. Like most of us, he got on, looked up at the numbers, punched his in and looked down at the floor. He never once glanced at me. Perhaps he didn't want to put a convict on the spot, seeing the handcuffs and the marshals and all. Like most of the public, he just looked away.

When my case was called, the judge simply shook his head. "You represent one of the saddest cases I have ever tried." He noticed my hand and mentioned the gunshot. "Do you have anything to say?"

I shook my head no.

He sentenced me to two years on each count, all to run concurrently with my state sentence. This was a huge plus for me, one of those positive *why me* moments. It effectively ended my federal commitment when my state time was complete. I thanked him.

He wished me a better rest of my life and then I was escorted out of the court.

The bus ride back to Terminal Island and the rest of my stay with the feds was uneventful. I left the federal penitentiary within a matter of days. The marshals who transported me back to CRC treated me very well. We made small talk along the way. They were familiar with my cases, and at one point even offered to stop at a roadside winery and buy me a drink.

I thanked them, but refused. There was so much more at stake now—my salvation. I was saved and could feel the presence of the Lord from the top of my head to my toes. It was a good feeling. There was so much to look forward to and to be thankful for. Maybe one day, I would even write a book.

THE BIRTH OF NONAME

B Y THE TIME I got back to my dorm, it was time to be assigned to a bottom bunk. When the cast was taken off, I had been moved to an upper bunk. I was moved a short distance from King, within shouting distance.

My bunkie on the left was named Squirrel; he was a die-hard Blood from Pasadena. He loved to talk and I was a good listener. The first thing he asked was my name.

"I don't have a name." I explained that I had just returned from court, which he knew, but we hadn't had a chance to meet. We went back and forth with this name thing. Finally I told him to call me NoName (since I was giving up my ties to the past).

He was a youngster and he seemed to enjoy this, so NoName it was. When any of his homies came by to visit, he introduced me as such.

I've never looked a squirrel straight in the face, so I'm not sure whether he was called Squirrel because of his looks or because of his personality. I did find out that he braided hair and was willing to do mine for a pack of smokes whenever I needed it. I agreed.

Squirrel fell in love with my daughter when he first saw a picture of her. He couldn't believe I had a daughter that old. I politely told him that she wasn't that old, only seventeen, and definitely not a match for him.

Squirrel was so caught up in the red versus blue thing that when I got a package from home that included a blue head band he stopped braiding my hair. I literally had to throw it in some bleach water to turn it some weird purple color before I was okay again.

On my left was another young black named Dilbert. His claim to fame was that he said he was the nephew of George Foreman, the heavyweight boxing champion. Looking at him, it was believable. He had a big round face, just like George. He claimed to be from Texas, as was George. He had a Texas twang to go along with the face. So who knew? Dilbert was a coffee drinker and would talk your ear off after having a cup.

Once I met Squirrel, it seems I began to meet all the youngsters in the dorm. There was Nut, a Crip. He and Squirrel got along, when they did, only because circumstances dictated it. On the outside, they would be sworn enemies. Sam and Hercules worked out every day and had the build to prove it. There were many others, black, brown, and white, who I was destined to spend the next two years of my life with.

Perhaps NoName carried some sort of spiritual connotation. Maybe it was me letting go of the past, bringing nothing, not even my name with me. But this couldn't have been what it was all about. Some inmates already knew my name before I decided not to tell Squirrel. I guess I just saved NoName for Squirrel and the younger brothers.

These brothers actually flung around the so-called N-word brazenly. The word was so ingrained in them that I don't think they could speak a sentence without using it. NoName was kind of my way of not identifying with what they stood for.

These youngsters were hardline Bloods and Crips. In many cases, these young men would be willing to die to show their allegiance to the gang that had become family. They made no bones about their dislike of each other. They wore their CK (Crip Killer) and BK (Blood Killer) tattoos with pride.

It was all the older brothers could do just to keep them in check long enough to get them to see that their fighting each other weakened blacks throughout the prison system. It was the age-old tale—as long as blacks did in other blacks, the opportunity for other races to overcome us was made that much simpler. Our penchant for holding each other back gives clear opportunity to stay behind as a group. It's a unique situation that perhaps only blacks understand—but fall prey to anyway.

I've never considered myself a racist. My upbringing was all black, but as a kid I didn't feel the results of discrimination. I can only remember one time as a youngster seeing discrimination in action. I was staying with my cousins in Buffalo, New York, one summer. My father's brother was their dad; their mom was Japanese. Both of my cousins looked Japanese. I already was several shades lighter than most blacks, and when I was younger, my hair even had a blondish tint—but don't tell anyone.

One day my two half-black, half-Japanese cousins, my cousin Junior—who was as black as they come—and I decided to go swimming. After we had been in the pool awhile, Junior was asked to get out. The rest of us got out too, although we weren't asked. We all went home together, and that was the end of it. I don't even think we told our parents.

The young black crowd of today or back in my day, too, couldn't or wouldn't identify racial degradation with calling each other a nigga. We had no respect for what our forefathers had gone through to stop the use of that name. Oh yeah, we marched the marches and shouted black power, but when we were alone we were as nigga as a nigga could be. For some reason it wasn't until I got to prison and listened to some of my older cellmates that I realized the irony of it all. We would be willing to fight someone from another race who used the term, but it was okay for us to use it and set that example for our children.

When I left my black neighborhood to attend a nearly all-white college—there were nine blacks in my freshman class of thousands at Drexel University in 1969—it shocked my socks off. It wasn't that I was discriminated against. It was the cultural shift, which I had never experienced. I wasn't used to being around that many white folks.

I actually had a marketing professor use the N-word in my presence. Somehow, he worked it into the subject matter of the day. Me being the only black, I felt about two inches tall. He was a good ole boy and had the southern drawl to prove it.

In a Communications class, as a class project I designed a collage. All it contained was one black face, surrounded by hundreds of white ones. That collage sent a message. I got an "A".

In prison, NoName wanted to send a message. Cut it out. Band together. It was tough enough being in prison without worrying about your colors or sets. Did I get my point across? No. Would I do it again? Yes, and then not wait thirty years to write a book to explain it.

So I proudly wore the tag NoName. When Squirrel left for the streets, he gave me the mattress that he had treasured for so long. It was bonnaroo, as they say in New Orleans—best on the street. A real mattress, not one of the flattened ones the CDC gave out. When I left, I gave it to an old white guy who must have been in his sixties who I had trained to take my place at the warehouse. Now that's progress, wouldn't you say?

On the Mexican side I met Poncho, Angel, and some others whose names are too numerous to recount. The only white boy in the dorm that I grew attached to was named Sammy. He slept in bunk one, right next to the CO's office, the telephone, and the coffee pot. The remarkable thing about Sammy was that his hair was completely gray. He wasn't that old, maybe early-to-mid thirties, but word had it that he was doing so much hard time his hair just turned gray. By "hard time," people meant that he missed home so much and talked on the phone so much that he never adjusted to prison life. He was miserable and looked it. Talk about Eeyore the donkey—he definitely fit that bill.

Chilly was a brother in his early thirties who spent much of his time in the TV room watching soaps. He was the one who worked in the kitchen and would hook me up with an extra piece of meat when the menu had fried chicken or pork chops. He also gave me Jheri curls when my hair needed a remake.

There were many others who came and went. The turnover wasn't as frequent as at the county jail. In prison we got to know each other over years, not months. Most of the guys I met outside the dorm were Christian brothers I met through Mr. Smith or King.

There was one, however, whose name also stuck with me. We called him Philly, because that's where he was from. I identified, because I had spent five years in the City of Brotherly Love while in college.

Philly had lived in Pomona immediately preceding his arrest. His arrest was rather complicated. He had a federal charge for some crime he never disclosed. He also had a state charge for beating his girlfriend. "I didn't really beat her," Philly claimed. "I just started tapping on her while we were having sex; it was as good for her as it was for me." He described it as a spanking which they both agreed to as part of their sex lives, but I guess the young lady—who was old enough, but not old enough for Philly as far as her mom was concerned—changed her testimony in court. Philly was still appealing his sentence and firmly believed he would be released soon.

The federal crime was more of a parole violation. For some reason, unlike me, he decided to roll the dice and assumed that the feds would not pick him up once he was released from the state.

Philly was a gambler and ran a football sports book out of Dorm 51, the "old man's dorm." He always got on me about having my hair done or Jheri curled. He was a fan of the natural and felt we all should be. Philly had no use for God, and I cannot recall him ever mentioning the Lord while we were down. He stayed away from our Bible studies. He held a large stash of pornographic magazines including, I was told, some pictures of his lady friend. He would rent them out.

He was also a clerk in the captain's office and eventually found out that one of his Pomona home girls was a correctional officer (CO) at CRC. This did not work in his favor.

During the fall of 1987, Philly took a huge hit on his football bank. He lost so much that he was borrowing packs of cigarettes from all of us to pay off the debt. As mentioned earlier, cigarettes were the prison currency at the time. One pack generally represented one dollar and

The Birth of NoName

Camels were the brand of choice. We didn't gamble, but I understood the problem. He could get shanked over something like this. I gave him what I had, even drawing down money from my books to purchase more cigarettes. It wasn't enough, though, and Philly did the unthinkable. He contacted his home girl CO, who worked on the women's unit, and asked her to help him out. She immediately reported it. Philly lost his job and got a 115 write-up on top of it.

Doing special favors, particularly ones like giving an inmate material things were severe violations and could cost the CO. their job. Depending on the level of the favor (bringing in drugs or contraband for example) could also lead to legal problems for both the inmate and the CO.

There were two types of disciplinary write-ups an inmate could get: a 128B and a 115, named after the forms they were written on. A 115 was the more severe of the two and could lead to a loss of privileges, like visits or packages, all the way up to receiving additional time. These write-ups could also hinder transfers to lower-lever prisons.

It was not a good time for him.

101

HAVIN' CHURCH

GOD IS EVERYWHERE. There's no greater testament to this than the services held within the prison walls across the country. I quit smoking in May 1986, in order to prepare myself to either work or volunteer in the chapel. Work numbers were limited, and as Mr. Smith said it, many of the inmate staff at the chapel bickered and fought so much, it caused you to question their salvation. It reminds me of today's churches, too.

Oops, did I say that?

I applied to be a volunteer usher, anyway. I was interviewed by the chaplain and the inmate staff and had no problem getting a position. I just had to be loyal and on my post for my assigned services. There wasn't much to it. We rotated around the sanctuary and stood available if anyone had a question or if any of the outside guests had a need. We also took count at each service. There were slips that an inmate could fill out to have money taken out of his money draw account, so we actually took offering. If the visiting churches brought in flyers or handouts, we distributed them to the congregation.

Naturally, everyone who came to the chapel did not come for the service. Because the COs kind of left the sanctuary off to itself, with minimal supervision, some inmates actually used the back pews to shoot up heroin, or have homosexual encounters. But where sin abounds, grace abounds even more, as the apostle Paul said, and

God always makes provision for those who want to hear the Word to receive it.

All of us had our favorites when it came to the visiting ministries. One of my favorites was Sister Norris and the group she brought from her church in Long Beach. She would always start off with a song that began, "Keep your mind on Jesus, we gonna have a time, keep your mind on Jesus, we gonna have a time, talkin' 'bout a real good time..."

These saints were Pentecostal, and although I had been brought up in a Baptist church, the Pentecostals seem to really have it going on. They would get to dancin' in the spirit and kickin' off their shoes and before you knew it the whole congregation was shoutin'.

Another of my favorites was a young man who had been incarcerated and came back to help others. I can't recall his name, I just remember his sincerity. His favorite song went like this: "Call Him up, call Him up, tell him what you want, all you got to do is call Him up..."

I got to the point where I was loving the Lord more and more. We would make our way back to the dorm with fresh anointing, and boy did that feel good.

Another minister I was later to meet again on the outside was named King Johnson. He used an overhead projector and wrote what seemed like a thousand Scriptures up on the screen. Sometimes this got boring, because there was absolutely no singing, unless the inmate deacon who oversaw the service led us in song. King was a sincere man who really loved the Lord, and I was blessed to meet him outside the prison gates—it just so happened that he later married my daughter's mother in law.

Each denomination had its day to worship. So on some days there would be Catholic worship and other times there would be Muslim worship. Many brothers went to Muslim services, because they spoke of a way of life that was appealing to blacks. These were black Muslims, and the services were along the line of Louis Farrakhan and his followers. I don't recall going to any of the services, because although they presented good lifestyles, I didn't see the way to salvation. I not only wanted to live a good life, but I longed for the life after death that the Bible speaks of.

I must admit it was much easier to serve God while incarcerated, and we would hear this over and over again. Sayings to the effect that it's easy to serve God when you don't have any of the everyday temptations of the world. This was partially true. We knew where our next meal was coming from. If womanizing is your problem, no problem—get arrested and come to prison. We can take care of that for you. Drugs, theft—they were available, but the consequences could be even harsher than on the outside. It's easier to leave it alone when you're locked up.

BRO BOOKER SAYS...

Some might think they need to go to jail to get fixed, but I'm being satirical here. I wouldn't recommend that anyone violate the law to purposely end up in prison. There are just too many variables that could cause this decision to go terribly wrong, beginning with the commission of a crime. My experience turned out right because it was the path that God chose for me—it was His plan not mine. As I explain in the intermission chapter, if God wasn't directing the incidents in my life, there could have been consequences much worse than I suffered, up to and including death.

My hat goes off to those ministries who visit men and women in jails and prisons around the country. There is no great monetary reward. I can't see them being able to build a megachurch based on the incomes of the inmates. I was considered a highly paid inmate, and my tithes amounted to about $4 per month. That won't get them that organ or those new pews. The people who came to visit us did so because they felt led by God. The only rewards they expected were spiritual.

The chapel had its own little library of resources. There were cassette tapes and books available to check out at no cost. There were also a lot of mail-order Bible studies available for the asking.

And then there were people like Mama Ruth. She was based somewhere in or near Santa Barbara. All you had to do was write. She would share what God had done in her own life. The pictures she would send showed that life to be a meager one. Pictures of her dog and her husband. Pictures of other inmates who were writing. Testimonies.

Every time I wrote Mama Ruth with nothing more than a desire to say how much I appreciated her, she would send me a book of stamps. Now a book of stamps may not seem like much to most, but Mama Ruth knew what us inmates needed, and she went directly to the root of it. She was a Mexican woman, but never once did I hear her talk about the races. She was Mama Ruth, and I am sure that as I write this book, God has made a special place in His kingdom for people like her. People who were willing to give so much and yet ask for so little in return.

I wish I had followed the voice in my mind and attempted to locate her once I was released. Like many other "coulda wouldas" in my life, this was one that never got fulfilled.

I will never forget her.

CHEAP LABOR

IN THE CDC you are able to work days off your sentence. As long as you were working or attending school, you received one day off your sentence for every day. This is what we called half time. N-numbers and were two groups of inmates who did not qualify for half time.

Shortly after arriving at CRC, I met with my counselor. My release date of May 15, 1988 was calculated based on half time and the assumption that I would not receive any write-ups for bad behavior. Without going into great detail, an inmate could receive a 128B or a more severe 115 for certain violations of prison rules. In holding with my personality as pretty much a rule follower—except for the drugs and crimes that got me there—I can say that during my time in prison, I never received either of these disciplinary actions.

After meeting Mr. Smith, I'd decided that the ideal job would be in the chapel. Not only would I get workday credits, but I would be able to pray and study the Bible. These jobs were hard to come by, so the first job I got was that of a teachers' aide. I worked in an English as a Second Language class from the time I was first assigned a job until I went out to court to appear before the federal judge on my probation violation. All in all, I worked in this capacity for about four months. It was crazy.

The teacher was a state employee who didn't appear to have too much interest in accomplishing anything. The students, all Mexicans, were given workbooks, and they went through them at their own pace. I was paid the extraordinary amount of fifteen cents an hour to make myself available as far as assisting those who actually wanted to be assisted. Most didn't. The students got half time too, just for being there.

The important part of the job was earning the half time. The amount of money I made was really insignificant. It was put on my books and whenever the canteen was open to my unit, I could purchase necessities. Things for sale included cigarettes, rolling tobacco, toiletry items, and various snacks. Each inmate was given a fairly large locker in which to store their personal items, which included the canteen products, changes of clothes (should I wear jeans and a blue shirt or a blue shirt and jeans?) and anything we might have received in packages from our families.

This first job was about as unrewarding as the pay. The teacher sat at the front, took roll and pretty much checked out for the remainder of the day. The students laughed, joked, and spoke in Spanish most of the time, so I'm not sure what they got out of the class. I was just there, passing the time.

When I got back from my time at court, God blessed me to get a better job. It was not the highly desired job of working in the chapel, but it was a blessing nonetheless. After taking a typing test, I was hired by a state employee who doubled as a correctional officer part time, as well as supervisor of the warehouse annex for stationery supplies. There were only four of us working in the warehouse, and I served as the clerk, but also did shipping and receiving when needed. I was also in charge of the inventory.

This job actually paid forty-eight cents an hour, triple what I had been used to. Again, it wasn't the money, but the ability to work off my time. My supervisor, Dan, was a young white man and he meshed with us inmates very well. The guy who trained me was short to the house—that is, ready to go home. He was in the process of writing a book. A pornographic book. He felt led occasionally to read pages out loud to get feedback.

God has some kind of humor. I was able to pretty much ignore the trash that came with being incarcerated while upholding my manhood.

Because I still had about two years left to do, my supervisor considered me an ideal hire. In his mind, he wouldn't have to fit anyone else into the team for quite some time. I had great times on the job. Dan had one strict rule. Don't steal. There was hardly anything that we couldn't get if we asked him for it, but the key was to ask him.

Working in this warehouse came with many privileges. Because it contained basically stationery and cleaning products, we were very popular within our dorms. Even the COs would ask us to bring home items they may have had trouble getting: things like markers, notepads, pencils, or pens. The CDC accepted my warehouse job as far as my earning half-time. My position as an usher and later as a deacon were voluntary and not taken into account as far as CDC decisions were concerned. There were a few clerical jobs attached to the chapel, but these positions normally had long wait lists.

Dan would occasionally do special favors for us, too, like bringing in a dozen donuts or signing us out for lunch and ordering a pizza from the outside. One time, a twenty-five-inch TV was mistakenly delivered to our warehouse. Instead of sending it back, Dan helped us hook it into a cable line. We cut the top of the box it was delivered in and put it over the TV. This helped keep it secure and, to my knowledge, no one knew but the four of us inmates and Dan.

My co-workers were all white, but they treated me as one of the gang. Occasionally, they used the N-word, but would always excuse me from the conversation. For the most part, these guys were hardened convicts and had come down from higher-level penitentiaries like Folsom, San Quentin, and Soledad. It seemed they had been doing time all of their lives.

Bam Bam, Rattler, and Killjoy were the three that I worked with for the longest period of time. Killjoy and I were hired about the same time; the others came later. They would keep me up to date if something were about to jump off, especially if it was racial. Although we didn't have any Mexicans among our group, the white boys seemed to know when they were planning something.

Somehow, we managed to keep the great divide of our cultural backgrounds in check. As my wife will tell you today, I am an appeaser. So that was probably part of it, but the other part was that I had been broken down to the point to where nothing really seemed to faze me.

Even in the dorm, I got along with most everyone. Lockers were broken into almost on a daily basis, but never did it happen to me. God made sure I had the right people around me.

Many of the inmates looked down upon the Christians, mostly because some of them were so fake and the inmates could smell that a mile away. Somehow they knew I was sincere. Many of them—all races—would come to me with a prayer request or when they were leaving, would ask me to pray with them. I made no bones of getting down on my knees every night and when I was able to get a TV, the channel would usually be turned to Christian Broadcasting. All I wanted to do was to serve the Lord and one day get out of prison.

BOOKER SAYS ...

THERE'S A PSALM THAT ADVISES, "YE THAT LOVE THE LORD, HATE EVIL:" I DID.

THEN IT SAYS, "HE PRESERVETH THE SOULS OF HIS SAINTS; HE DELIVERETH THEM OUT OF THE HAND OF THE WICKED." AND HE CERTAINLY HAS BEEN DOING THAT.

(SEE PSALM 97:10)

KEEP THIS IN YOUR MIND AND LET IT GUIDE YOUR DAY.

As I said, life in our warehouse had its privileges. If the facility was on lockdown, Dan would come and get us so we could do our thing as if the day hadn't changed at all. However, lockdowns at CRC were still considered unusual, because the prison yard was a medium security environment.

One of the best parts of working there was making deliveries to the women's unit. Dan would get one of the open-bed trucks with wooden siding, and we would all pile in and prepare for the whistles and stares we got from the women as we made our way around their unit. There were even times he would let one of us drive.

Another thing about the warehouse was that we had our own private restroom. We didn't have to sit side-by-side, fifteen or twenty toilets, while others came in to wash their face or brush their teeth. Having our own restroom was truly a big, big deal.

Once a quarter we would shut down for our inventory. Dan prided himself on perfection, and so did I. Since the invoices and purchase orders were basically my responsibility, I really worked hard at getting things right. There were actually several times when we had perfect inventories, and Dan would treat us with pizza or donuts.

It was Dan who, during one of our trips to the women's unit, spied out the woman who would later be my wife.

BRO BOOKER SAYS...

There is another psalm that says, "O love the Lord, all ye his saints..." And I did.

Then it says, "...for the Lord preserveth the faithful, and plentifully rewardeth the proud doer." And if you ever meet me and my wife, you'll see that he has preserved both of us for him and each other in ways only a loving Father in heaven can. (See Psalm 31:23)

LOCKDOWN!

I CAN ONLY RECALL a few lockdowns at CRC. They came in all sizes. Sometimes only the dorm was on lockdown. One such occasion was when someone lit a book of matches and threw it in the direction of a rookie CO during count time. Thinking it was a firecracker or something, he took off running into the office to much laughter from the inmates. The unit lieutenant, however, didn't find it amusing. It was around Christmastime, and the first thing he saw when he stormed into the dorm was our makeshift Christmas tree. Straight in the trash can it went.

"Who threw the matches?" he demanded.

No one was going to snitch. As I found out in the county jail, that was one thing that stood above most others as far as what not to do. It just wasn't going to happen, and I'm sure he knew it.

We were all told to undress down to our shorts and sit on our bunks. The normal lockdown protocol.

The lieutenant stormed up and down the dorm ranting and raving like the mad man that he was. Many years after Mr. Smith and I got out—we kept in touch—we referred to this gentleman as Mad Dog.

He threatened to put the whole dorm on the transportation list and send us off to parts unknown, getting us so lost in the system that it would take weeks for the CDC to straighten things out. By the time we got back, our bunks and personal items would be lost in the sauce.

He canceled our yard, canteen, visits, and mail.

That did it. The guilty party quickly owned up to his action. I'm sure he didn't receive any more than a 115. He was back with us in a few days. It took that CO, though, a while longer to face us—not that any of us would have had the nerve to bring it up again.

The worst lockdown I experienced came about when two young blacks were playing catch football and happened to hit an older Mexican with the ball. Not only did they not apologize, but they insulted him by calling him old and asking, "What are you gonna do anyway?"

Dumb question.

Other Mexicans got in on the fray.

The blacks on the yard knew these two young brothers had disrespected the man.

Sometime later in the day, I saw two young Mexicans come into our dorm through the side door and go straight into the restroom. They peeled off their bloody shirts and tossed them into a trash can. They then went to the sinks and washed thoroughly.

One of them was one of our dorm members. He saw me watching. I saw him watching me.

Dang, I had just given this guy a shot of Kool-Aid a day or two ago.

He jumped on his bunk, and the other guy went back out the side door.

I put down my book as my stomach fluttered a bit. It was about to be on.

Within minutes, there was a clear-the-yard siren. All inmates were to report to their dorms for count. Once we were counted, we were told to strip down to our shorts and stand in front of our bunks.

Several COs went up and down the dorm and checked each one of us for cuts or scratches. They even looked under our fingernails for blood. I later found out that the same process went on throughout the prison. I also learned that two blacks had been shanked in the dorm next to ours. One was in really bad shape.

The ironic part was that the one in the worst shape—near death—hadn't even been involved in the earlier incident. He happened to see what was going down and tried to get between the stabber and the intended victim. He was just trying to break it up.

This lockdown shut down everything. Visiting was closed, and so were most jobs and classes. The yard was closed.

Lockdown status for meals meant each dorm was escorted by five or six deputies to the dining room. The dorm ahead of us would be escorted out when we went in. I guess it took most of the day just to feed us all three meals.

Each dorm had a dorm representative for the primary races. The dorm reps met with other dorm reps throughout the facility. This lockdown went on for approximately three or four days before staff was confident enough to allow some privileges back.

It was a while before things got totally back to normal. I know that at least one of the culprits wasn't caught, but I had trained myself long ago to keep my mouth shut and my eyes and ears open. If you minded your own business and stayed away from gambling and sex, you could pretty much do your time without incident.

Of course, if there came a time to stand up for yourself, you stood up. My motto was, if it wasn't something that I had to deal with personally, then it wasn't worth putting my time on the line. I never even mentioned what I had seen to King or Mr. Smith.

During this lockdown, Dan came and got me for work. When I got to the warehouse with the other guys it was business as usual.

I never opened my mouth.

BOOKER SAYS...

Sharing our faith is a process. Some are designated to plant a seed, some water the seed, some fertilize it and God causes it to grow. When it comes to speaking out when you see a wrong being committed in prison, you have to use good judgment because prisoner confrontations can lead to severe consequences, even death. In many situations all you can do is pray that God give you an opening to plant a seed by sharing your own life experience or a deep question. That is what I prayed for in this case and others related to drug use or homosexual activity.

My first pastor after being saved always told us to look for things we had in common when sharing our faith. Start there and build on the conversation. It would be foolish to start out on an issue that I knew would be divisive. For example, I would rather ask someone,

"Do you believe that there is a power out there that is greater than yourself?"

vs.

"You're on your way straight to hell if you keep having sex outside of marriage!"

A NOTE FROM HEAVEN

MAIL CALL IN the prison system was one of the highlights of the day for many inmates. However, I suppose that for some, it was just a reminder that no one really cared. Most of the inmates I hung around with, the older guys, had already been down for several years. The only letters they might get would be official ones. Philly, for instance, was waiting on a response on an inquiry regarding the computation of his release date. Mr. Smith was expecting some type of compensation because he had worked many years in the naval ship yards and been exposed to asbestos. Some awaited word of money being placed on their books.

And then there were those like Dilbert, who wrote to every woman whose address he could get his hands on. Me, on the other hand, I just waited for return letters from friends and family members whom I had written to. I really appreciated letters that included photos.

When I first arrived at CRC, letters could be exchanged between the men's and women's units with no postage. All you needed was the name and CDC number. I vaguely remember writing someone a few times as a pen pal. I don't even remember how I got her name. I do remember it didn't last long, as we had little in common.

But Dilbert would write a woman as soon as he got hold of a movement sheet which showed names and CDC numbers. However, somewhere along the line, free mail to the women's unit stopped. Dilbert's writing nearly stopped too, but every now and then he would ask me how to spell a word or, more directly, ask me for a stamp, and then I knew Dilbert was at it again.

It was August, 1987. Mail call had just ended and Dilbert had gotten a letter. At first he was so excited I couldn't even tell what he was saying. Dilbert was extremely short. I don't think he reached more than five feet tall. He had already drunk some coffee and that always got his adrenaline going.

He walked swiftly up and down the center aisle of the dorm, talking swiftly and using the combination dialects of prison, black, and Texas that only Dilbert had a handle on. After only a few minutes he seemed disappointed. He just couldn't believe his luck. When he finally got a letter from one of the women on the hill, she was a Christian. Imagine that. He complained that she talked about God all the way through the letter.

He wanted one of those letters like Chilly would get, where the girls talked dirty. One of them even sent Chilly some snippets of her pubic hair. Chilly would pull it out of his locker every so often, sniff it, and then look at us and laugh. That's the kind of letter Dilbert longed for.

But it was not to be. At least not this time. After reading the letter over and over again, the only thing he seemed to enjoy was his name in the heading.

Dilbert threw it over on my bunk. "Here, you take it. You write her. All she talks about is Jesus, and that's pretty much all you talk about."

The letter sat there until after chow. When I came back, I picked it up.

It would change my life forever.

The letter to Dilbert was written by Debbie Black. He was right, she really seemed to love the Lord. Every other sentence was a Scripture or a Scripture reference. I just loved it. She was so on fire for the Lord.

I couldn't resist the opportunity to write her back. I took my time, wanting to make sure my words expressed my thoughts. I just wanted to talk to someone who kind of knew where I was coming from. I finished the letter and sent it off.

A week or so later, I received an answer. A letter from Debbie. It feels just like yesterday, but it's been twenty-six years since that letter. How do I know? Well, because I can hear her now in our home. Her laughter on the phone as she speaks to a client in her office, conducting her real estate business. I seldom call her Debbie. She's Debra to me. Debra Ann when I'm really trying to get her attention. As of this writing, we will have been married twenty-five years on December 10.

But hey, I've gotten way ahead of myself. Let me get back to the story and enjoy the courtship appropriately.

Debbie and I wrote each other at least once a week. She was originally from Palm Springs. I told her about my three children and one grandchild. She told me about her little boy. I wrote a couple of sentences about the kids' mother and the fact that, with Mr. Smith's help, I was seeking a divorce. I saw on a TV program that that's really a bad pick-up line but it was true, and at the time I wasn't trying to pick up on her.

Most of all, we talked about God, just like Dilbert said we would.

Like me, Debbie spent a lot of time in the chapel. We talked about our favorite visiting ministries. Many of the same ministries went to the women's unit as well as the men's unit.

We discussed our favorite Scripture verses and what they meant to us. Hers was Psalm 107. It speaks mostly about the number of opportunities God gave His people, Israel, to repent and how stubborn they were in that they fell back into the same sinful patterns not long after. My favorite Scripture, and it remains so to this day, is Philippians 4:6–9. These verses describe the apostle Paul's instruction to Christians to stop worrying and to grab hold of the peace of God, which is beyond human understanding.

Soon we were able to exchange photos. You could take photos on the yard on certain days. They were Polaroid, so you got them right away. I was in luck. When I sent her my picture, she didn't stop writing.

When she sent me hers, I was slightly surprised. She was black. For some reason, I thought Palm Springs was full of white people. I was thrilled that she was black. Now we had even more in common.

Soon Debbie's letters began coming with the hint of perfume.

My good friend King awakened me early one morning with the news that he was being transferred to Tehachapi to serve out the rest of his sentence. It's amazing how God orchestrates your life if you allow him to do so. It seems that Debbie's letters of encouragement came right around the time of King's transfer. I sort of lost a brother and gained a sister. Not only that, but King and I had somewhat slacked off on our persistence in Bible study, allowing checkers and cards to take away from our enthusiasm for the Word. King's leaving and Debbie's letters helped me to get back on track spiritually—and that's why God put me here in the first place.

I spent more time in the chapel and reading Debbie's encouraging letters to Mr. Smith. He loved to smell the perfume. I think it made him work harder on my divorce paperwork too. He loved the fact that Debbie and I seemed to be getting serious.

Debbie was a clerk in the women's sewing center. I showed her picture to everyone I knew, even Dan. One day, Dan told us he was going to get the truck. We all knew what that meant. We were going up the hill to the women's unit. When he got back with the truck, we had even remembered to fill the orders from up there and have the supplies pulled and ready at the loading dock. We loaded the truck, jumped in, and off we went.

I rode shotgun. The others were in the flatbed, flexing their muscles while somehow trying to be nonchalant about it all. We made our way around the track and up the winding road to Administration and the women's unit.

After delivering the supplies, we were sitting in the truck waiting to pass through the gate and make our way back to the warehouse.

Dan tapped me on the shoulder. "There's the lady you've been writing."

I looked into the sea of women who just happened to be congregating at the gate as the studs prepared to make their way back down the hill. I didn't see her.

Dan pointed her out again.

I didn't think the one he pointed to was Debbie.

"Look at that smile," Dan said. "That's definitely her."

I looked again, staring hard.

She waved a bookmark shaped like a bear. It was the one I had sent her which said "Everything Is Bearable with Jesus."

It was her! We had finally met face to face.

VISITING

MY FAMILY DIDN'T yet know about Debbie. I wasn't sure if even telling them during a visit would be a good idea. Visiting within the state prison system was what we called "contact visits." This meant that, unlike at the county jail, you were no longer separated by a glass window and speaking through a telephone.

The visiting room was furnished with tables and chairs, and you could actually greet your visitors with a hug or handshake. Every now and then a CO would have to separate a couple who might be going at it a little too hot and heavy. Although kissing was allowed, you couldn't get carried away. I didn't have that problem, since my visitors were not of that nature. There were snack machines, and visitors could buy cigarettes for you to take back to your dorm.

Once I got to my permanent housing, visits were allowed every day. However, for someone to visit they had to be approved by you and the CDC System. There was a form they had to complete and submit. Children could only visit when accompanied by their legal guardian. Fortunately, in my case that was my mom. Once a year there would be a custody hearing that I was invited to attend under the supervision of the CDC. I always refused. My mom's place was the best place for them.

You couldn't have braids when you went out to visit, so I would always have them taken out beforehand. Once I started getting my hair curled, it didn't matter.

Inmates had to go through the strip-search process on the way back in. The CDC also reserved the right to strip-search visitors at the prison's discretion.

I had a very close friend, Harold, who had a criminal record and told me in his first letter not to expect any visits because of that. He didn't want to go through the strip-search process, and I don't blame him. Harold later told me that when he heard I had been shot and arrested for armed robbery, he immediately checked himself into a drug rehab. He put together several years of sobriety after that. He said my personality just didn't fit the crime, and if drugs had taken me that far out of my nature, he realized the potential downside of using them.

I did have one cousin who came with other members of our family, including her mom, my dad's sister, who had traveled all the way from Cleveland. They pulled my cousin out of line for a strip search and she refused. Her record was squeaky-clean, so I don't know what profile she fit, but I didn't blame her for refusing to go through the process. She waited in the parking lot until my visit was over.

I recall one unexpected visit. His name was Howard. We had worked together as special agents at the IRS. He'd been a good friend and even loaned me money just as my life was going up in flames. He had since changed jobs and at the time was working as a security agent for NASA.

He visited early one afternoon, and I was never exactly sure why he came. I think he wanted to see for himself if I was actually there and hear my story. Since he wasn't on my visiting list, I guess he just showed his badge and they let him in. When I saw him I was pleasantly surprised, but embarrassed that he was seeing me in that position. It was bad enough, the way I had fallen from grace with the IRS, but to have fallen this far was really disastrous.

There was another type of visit inmates could receive. They were called conjugal or family visits. The inmates had other names for them, more descriptive of the planned activity. This visit lasted from Friday evening until Sunday morning. It was usually your wife, and you had to have a marriage certificate to prove it.

I had two family visits during my stay—none, naturally, with my wife. Both were with my mom, kids, and granddaughter. I was taken up the hill to Administration. There I met my family and had an apartment for the weekend. The family brought food. One time my auntie even made chitlins for my mom to bring. We would watch TV, play games, and enjoy family time together. There was a playground for the little ones. I really looked forward to these, but two was enough. I found out what the old timers already knew: anything that disrupted your program made doing time harder.

The last visit I recall getting was from my daughter. It was in March or April of 1988, and I was just about ready to leave. She had just turned eighteen and was able to visit on her own.

Bridgette was the apple of my eye, and she knew it. Her daughter, Portia, now three years old, was a close second. "Granddad, just what type of apartment is this, anyway?" she asked on that afternoon.

During this visit, Bridgette put on her big-girl hat to give Daddy some advice. "Do not get out and go back to my mother."

She described going to her mom's place and seeing a man's shoes under the bed. She said the drugs and all the lunacy that came with them were still a big part of her mom's life.

I told Bridgette about Debra. Our relationship had grown strong, and I had started the process of filing for a divorce, after consulting my Bible and some of the brothers who were seasoned in the Word, to ensure that divorce was something I could do under God's grace. I told Bridgette it had gotten pretty serious, and that Debra was scheduled to be released just a week after I was.

Bridgette seemed relieved. I think this bit of information took a load off her mind.

SATAN CALLS AGAIN

I T WAS ALMOST Christmas, 1987. My relationship with Debbie had continued to blossom. There had even been a couple more times when we had been able to see each other close up. Two or three times, Dan had made arrangements for us to deliver supplies to the women's sewing center ourselves, instead of just dropping them off on the unit.

I was really short to the house now. Once we entered 1988, it would only be a matter of months. My original date of May 15 had been bumped back to May 20 due to my going out to federal court. Debbie's release date was May 25, just five days after mine.

There's an old saying among Christians that goes something like: When God has a blessing, Satan starts to messing.

It was just a simple twist while I was taking a shower. I almost slipped and grabbed hold of the faucet to avoid falling. I felt a slight twinge in my back. Within a week, I was having difficulty walking. I made my way to sick call and they gave me a couple of Tylenol and a crutch. They also gave me an off-work order, which I refused to even turn in to the dorm CO or to Dan.

I made my way to the warehouse every day, slowly but surely. I sat down a lot and described my injury as slight to Dan. He excused me from lifting. However, I began to walk slower and slower. I was having so much trouble that I actually got turned back a couple of times for arriving at chow more than two dorms after ours was called. The guys in the dorm understood, though, and besides Chilly, Dilbert, and Squirrel, even some of the Mexicans and whites brought me stuff to eat. Plus I had canteen and stuff leftover from packages in my locker. Jehovah-Jireh, which means God my Provider.

Worse, though, I started to miss church services because I couldn't walk the distance to the chapel in time. Finally it all came down on me at once. I woke up one morning and couldn't move my legs at all. I told my bunkie, who told the CO, who was new to the dorm and did nothing. Finally at 4 p.m. count I told one of the regular COs who had been in the dorm for some time. He knew I wasn't the type to call false alarms. He called the prison paramedics—inmates—who took me to the infirmary.

I spent several days in the infirmary, including Christmas. I remember thinking it was really a bummer, not only being in prison on Christmas, but being in the infirmary on top of it. I did get visits from the deacons in the ministry for visiting the sick, which, ironically, I was also a part of. They would come and pray with those who requested it.

When I was first asked to be part of this team during the summer of 1986, only six months after I became an usher, I was hesitant. I was assigned to the "Hospital Ministry." This required going into the prison infirmary and praying for those inmates. I didn't particularly care to be around sick folk. However, the Protestant inmate leader who made the request said maybe I should try to do something that I wasn't comfortable doing. Maybe that's the way God would have it. Weren't we all called to sacrifice? How could I refuse? So I accepted and actually got ministered to by them.

I began my stay in the infirmary in terrible pain. The nurse could tell I wasn't acting and got authorization from one of the doctors to begin giving me pain shots. The shots definitely eased the pain. I think I had started to get used to the medication because all I wanted to do was lay in bed until it was time for my shot. Meals were brought in, and when I was in the room by myself—there were two beds per room—I had free rein of the TV.

I must have been in the infirmary for about one week. When I got back to the dorm, everything was as usual. The COs had moved my locker into their office for safekeeping. Since I was able to walk normally, I just went right back to my normal routine. Once again Satan had been defeated, and I had been strengthened through the prayer and encouragement of others.

When I got my mail, I found that Debbie had sent me some chocolate, courtesy of a See's Candies drive available to inmates. I also received Christmas cookies and a little handmade Christmas card from one of the children at the Crystal Cathedral—something they did for every inmate at CRC.

God proved that He was still in control.

Although I saw the doctor once or twice while I was in the infirmary, it was not until several years later that I found out what the diagnosis was. About two months before my release I was sent to the hospital for an MRI. The results were never released to me.

Three years after my release, I was involved in an auto accident. When I informed the doctor that there had been a prior back injury, one thing led to another. They obtained from Riverside County Hospital my medical records, which indicated that while in prison I had been diagnosed with a herniated disc.

The diagnosis didn't affect the case, but my attorney, who was an old friend, told me that the fact I had been in prison was going to be a problem. Sure enough, even though the accident was proved to be the other driver's fault, the settlement offered me was laughable. I took my attorney's advice and accepted it.

I went on with my life from there, but throughout post-prison life, I have found that although God forgives, many people don't. Several decisions would go against me based upon my record. However, all I need do is remind myself of the goodness of God revealed in my life's testimony since the arrest.

SAYING GOODBYE

I WAS GETTING CLOSER and closer to going home. Mr. Smith had a release date a little over a month before me. He was beyond excited.

I started to walk the track with him when he went on check-out status in March, meaning for the thirty days before leaving, he had a free pass to the yard and chapel. Since we were in different units, I could only walk the track on certain days, but now he could go with me and we could walk and talk the Scripture.

When possible, I would go with him when he delivered the chapel flyers. Squirrel had discharged and left me his mattress. Dilbert and most of the other guys were still there.

Since having the cast removed nearly two years before, I had begun to work out at the weight pile during my free time. I also did push-ups in the back of the warehouse, and whenever I lost a game of dominoes to a newfound older friend named Mickie. As a result, I was getting pretty muscular. I was approaching thirty-seven years of age, but probably in the best shape of my life. Even during my football-playing days, I had smoked cigarettes. Not anymore.

As a deacon at the chapel, I taught a Bible study to anyone who could come. I was also the inmate host for a couple of services a month. If the outside ministry failed to show up, the deacon in charge was responsible for conducting the service. That meant I would prepare to minister whenever I had that responsibility, since I didn't want to be caught unprepared.

I got the opportunity to do this on a few occasions. It was scary at first, especially if it came on a Saturday night when we usually had the biggest outside ministries. The chapel would be packed, and then to have to get up in their place . . . it wasn't a comfortable feeling. However, this experience would benefit me greatly on the outside. If you could stand before prison inmates, many of whom didn't want to be there, you could probably stand before most others who actually wanted to hear the Word of God.

At the warehouse, I began training my replacement. John was a much older white guy from my dorm. I had told Dan about him, and when Dan saw that he still had years left to do, he was all for it. He couldn't be depended on to do much lifting, but he would keep the records straight and was a fairly good typist.

I have never met anyone who could type numbers on a typewriter as quickly and accurately as Dan. For a bow-legged white boy, he turned out to be a blessing in my life. He didn't realize it then, and neither did I until he pointed out Debra to me, but God really used him in my life. He even got me started listening to The Wave 94.7, the smooth jazz station I still listen to today, when I'm not listening to gospel.

Finally it was time for Mr. Smith to go. We continued to communicate after I was released. Mom and I went to see him when I first got out, and Mr. Smith gave me $100. Wow. He also considered himself having a crush on my mother, which I dismissed as infatuation. It's been several years now, and Mr. Smith and I have fallen out of touch. On the morning of his discharge, I walked him to R&R.

There was another inmate that I had grown really attached to. He was a younger brother who had come down from Soledad and had been shot on the yard while there. He was shot in the leg while he was lying on the ground, as we are all instructed to do if shots have to be fired from the gun tower. These were supposed to be warning shots to break up a fight between inmates. His name was Ted. The difference between Ted and most of the other younger brothers was that Ted loved the Lord. He was the first person I remember seeing take off running around the chapel when the Holy Ghost would grab hold of him.

Ted's other passion was weight lifting. About a year before he was scheduled to leave in late 1988, he gave up weight lifting to devote more time to God. He announced it one evening at chow, and I can remember the looks around the table. Ted stop lifting weights? You had to know him to realize the sacrifice this was, and he continued his commitment until I left, and probably until he left, too.

CHECK-OUT STATUS

FINALLY I REACHED check-out status. I was thirty days from leaving. When your name appeared on check-out status, you were given a new card that carried certain privileges. As it had for Mr. Smith, it gave me the freedom to go to the chapel or the main yard whenever they were open.

I particularly enjoyed going to the chapel in the early afternoon. It was pretty much deserted at that time except for the workers. The chapel was located at a far end of the prison right underneath a gun tower. There was a barbed-wire fence separating the prison from society. It was covered with a tarp, but you could see shadow through it and hear voices. You could see silhouettes of horseback and bicycle riders as they traveled the road outside.

It was surrealistic, knowing that just on the other side of this fence life went on as usual. I used to get the same feeling when I was at Chino West. There you could look out over the prison yard and see in the distance Central Avenue, one of the main streets in Chino. The buses and cars were going up and down the street as if everything was normal, and it was—for them. How many times had I driven down Central Avenue as a free man and looked up at the guard towers and not given a single thought about the people behind those fences and bars? I'd never driven through Norco, but my thoughts were the same. I was very close to being back out there.

Not long after I reached check-out status, I met with my counselor. I hadn't had an opportunity or need to meet with her except one other time. A little over a year prior, she had told me that, due to my good behavior and work, my points had dropped to eleven. That meant I qualified to go to a level-one or minimum-security yard.

When I'd first been arrested I thought level one was ideal. With a level-one status, the prison yard was far less restrictive than level two or above. Level-one inmates were the ones assigned to fire or road-work crews. They actually went out and mingled with free men. They were almost treated as free, maybe even getting a beer after putting out a fire or something, *Shawshank Redemption* style. But naturally I didn't qualify initially, and then when I did, I didn't want it.

I'd also thought about applying for a halfway house when I got within six months of my release date. These places were just like their name inferred. You were halfway out but also still halfway in. After seeing the consequences of several people I knew that went out to halfway houses, my thoughts about them changed quickly. Most returned with a violation or, worse, a new crime. Many returned with time added to their sentence. I guess there was just too much temptation. You had the freedom to leave, but there was a curfew. There was actually a CO on duty at the house and most of the violations seemed to be from going AWOL or giving a dirty drug test. It wasn't that I planned on going out and using, but, I made up my mind that I was better off where I was. Who was to say that God didn't want me to stay here for my allotted time, until He fixed things on the outside. That's how I came to look at it. When I was ready, God would see to my release, which just happened to be when I was scheduled to be released. No Get Out of Jail Free cards for me.

At that time, I just asked my counselor to do what she could to keep me right here at CRC. Besides, if I had left, I'd never have met Debra. So when I met with the counselor that last time, she just wanted to know what my plans were and where I would be staying. I told her I planned to work once released and that I'd be staying with my mom and children.

I was one of the fortunate ones—I actually had someplace to go. I felt for the ones who didn't. All they had was $200 in "gate money" and somehow they were supposed to make it. Talk about a setup for recidivism. Don't get me started.

At first the counselor suggested that going back to my old neighborhood was a bad idea. "Nothing's changed; same people, same places," she said.

I begged to differ. I had changed. I loved the Lord and He loved me. I refused to accept the idea that I could have gotten shot, gone through everything else I did, only for God to rescue me and then send me back on a one-way ticket to the joint.

Blank stare from her. "Okay, we're done here. Thank you." She smiled one of those, *I hear you, I've heard it before, but I've yet to see that work* type of smiles. She gave me the info I needed to contact my parole officer, which I had to do within twenty-four hours of my release.

And that was the last I saw of her. If I could remember her name, I'd mail a copy of my book to her and to that district attorney from my trial.

Another privilege I acquired on checkout was being relieved from work duty. This didn't work for me, so for the most part I continued to go up to the warehouse daily. Even though John was mostly trained, I had more freedom there than anywhere else on the yard. We still had our TV, and I got along well with the other three inmates. Even the salesmen who paid an occasional visit got to know me. In fact, once I was released and working, I happened to run into one of them at lunch. It was like old times, and he told me Dan and the guys were doing just fine.

I really enjoyed having more time to spend at the chapel. In the early afternoon it was cool and peaceful. I would sit in the pews and study my Bible, pray, or listen to the tapes they had in the library. I did a lot of praying.

One of the most important prayers to God concerned my

relationship with Debra. We both wanted to make sure we were doing the right thing. I had placed something called "fleeces" before God concerning my divorce. This idea of a fleece comes from the Bible, Judges 6:37–40, where Gideon tests God by using a literal fleece of wool to get an answer from God. In simple terms, a fleece attempts to get a yes or no answer from God by saying to him, "If this happens the answer is yes; if it doesn't happen, its no." The answer cannot be easy to obtain or it's not a sure sign from God.

At each step of the process I had asked God to stop it if divorce were not the right thing for me. When I was in the infirmary with my back injury, I had doubts. While there, I found a book by Chuck Swindoll that went into detail as far as when divorce was biblically appropriate. It was a small paperback, and I read it over a couple of times. When I was finished, I was convinced that my situation, based on my wife's infidelity alone, was enough for God to say, "Heck yeah, go for it, what took you so long?" My words, not His. The way things were turning out, it seemed God had approved, and the divorce would be official in June.

God was surely in it all along. When I mailed the paperwork to my uncle at my mom's house, it had to be served on my wife within a very short time. When he received the forms in the mail, it just so happened that she showed up at my mom's door the very same day. They hadn't seen her for weeks, but there she was appearing out of nowhere. Look at God work.

WHY ME?

Speaking of Chuck Swindoll, I just want to give a shout out for all of those radio and TV evangelists and ministries that make their way into the prison system. If I were to start naming them, I'm sure I would leave someone out, but they are all deserving of accolades. These ministries really kept me going. Not only the ministries, but the books, Bibles and Bible study correspondence that are mailed into the prisons, most times at no cost. Many times the books are written especially for those who are incarcerated. It's proof that God's Word is reaching in to the far corners of the earth, seeking those who are lost, and helping the blind to see. Hallelujah!

Soon I began my countdown: *Well this is the last week for laundry; this is the last month I have to put in for money draw; this is the last time I have to eat,* and so on.

I was so close to home cooking I could taste it.

THE GRAND FINALE

IT WAS THE day before *the day*. I spent most of it going around saying my goodbyes. There were even COs I needed to say goodbye to, such as Officer McCrary. He was the one who got me assistance when my back went out. When he saw me on the movement list, he told me that he mostly tells guys he'll see them again. But not me. He knew I was serious and not coming back. Well, he was half-right.

To date, I haven't gone back, although my plan has always been to join a prison ministry. Planting seed and gathering souls for Jesus. However, several years later, I was to meet Officer McCrary in another setting. He was in the lobby of the drug rehab I was working for. I had been on the job for a few years as the admissions coordinator, but I was moving on up, as they say. At first I could tell he didn't recognize me. Why would he, with the thousands of men who passed through his dorms between then and whenever he left? However, as I walked back through the lobby, he called out to me and shook my hand. He did remember. He remembered that I had been in at the same time as Nut, Stan, and Squirrel.

"You got it," I replied. "Remember the name?"

"No, no name, just the face" he said.

I smiled. "That's it." NoName. I gave him my card and helped give his parolee the red carpet treatment through the admission process.

Another officer I wanted to say goodbye to was one whose name

I can't recall. He knew the ones who were serious about Jesus, and several times when we passed him in the hallway, he would tell us to get up against the wall and assume the position. We would face the wall, spreading our arms, hands, legs, and feet. He would then fake the process of searching us, but all the time he would be laying hands on us and praying that the Lord watch over us. Wow.

I said my so-longs to Dan and the warehouse crew. I had given John my mattress a few days earlier. If anyone needed it, his old bones did. I made my way to the chapel and said goodbye to Chaplain Doughty and the inmate crew there.

After that, Ted and I just spent the rest of the day walking, talking, and praying.

Ted said he would be by to pick me up in the morning to walk me to R&R. "You'll probably have trouble sleeping tonight."

How wrong he was. When I made it back to the dorm after chow, I began to say my goodbyes to the guys there. I left some of them with personal things and canteen that I wouldn't be taking with me. I asked the black dorm representative to call a special meeting so I could pray. Most of the guys showed up. I talked to the brothers, telling them to watch out for themselves. Then I prayed and asked God to watch over them as only He can. I asked God to get them out of prison as soon as possible. The brothers laughed, we gave each other hugs, and that was that. I hit the sack and was out like a flash.

The next thing that I remember was Ted standing next to my bed. "It's time."

We made the walk up to the outside of R&R together. He could go no farther. Neither of us could hold back the tears as we gave each other one last hug.

When I got up to R&R I suddenly was filled with anxiety. *What if one of those other robberies that seemed so long ago happened to pop up in the computer? What if that traffic ticket I got in Vegas while working undercover for the IRS and had never paid came up in my name somehow, and there was a warrant for that?*

What if, what if, what if...

My mind didn't come to rest until they called my name. I was walked out to the sally port. The pedestrian gate was opened, and I could see my mom, Harold, and my grandbaby waiting for me.

As I hugged each one, the tears just gushed out. Harold asked if I was okay, and I finally managed to talk. "I'm okay, I'm okay, I'm okay." We got in the car and Harold drove off.

As we drove into Pomona, I told Harold and my mom that I wanted to stop at a local church that my mother, aunt, and uncle went to. I had gone there off and on before I was arrested. I remember my hypocrisy, as I would fire up a joint as soon as I drove off the parking lot, back in those days.

Harold, who was not saved, nor to my knowledge trying to be, asked me again if I was okay. They had planned a big barbecue for me at my mom's, and people were there waiting. I assured him that I was fine. I just wanted to pray. I needed to pray.

We pulled into the lot, and I got out and started pulling on the doors to get in, forgetting that it was the real world and things did get locked up on occasion. Some landscapers were working around the yard. I walked up to them and told them I really needed to get into the church to pray. They asked why. I told them I had just been released from prison and felt the urge of the Holy Ghost to pray. They went to get their boss.

He came out. "You mean you just got released?"

"I haven't even made it home yet," I explained.

He shook my hand. "Guys, open the door to the sanctuary."

In we went. I made my way to the altar and began to pray from the depths of my soul. My mother and granddaughter dropped to their knees too. I felt a sense of pride that someone had taught her to do this too. The landscapers, who were apparently church members there, prayed also.

Harold, on the other hand, came as far as the door but didn't step in.

Before I knew it, we were praying and began praising God and speaking in tongues. I really felt the presence of God. He dwells in the midst of praise.

When I was finally prayed out, I stood up. They stopped too. We walked back outside. The guys gathered around their supervisor, who had come back out to join us. Again, he asked, "Are you sure you just got out of the pen?"

"I'm sure." I replied. "My box with Bibles, letters, and stuff is right there in my friend's trunk."

The supervisor looked at me and shook his head. I guess this wasn't normal. "Well, if you just got out, you can't possibly have a job."

"That's right, I'm on my way home to my mom's for a cookout, and I haven't had time to think about a job yet," I replied.

"Well if you want to work here at the church, consider yourself employed!"

I didn't know what to say. Wow. I couldn't believe it. What if I hadn't asked Harold to stop? What if I had decided to wait until after the cookout to come here to pray?

Worse yet, what if I had left prison in the same shape that I entered, unsaved? What if, what if.

Why me, why me?

I do know one thing—at that precise moment my faith in God skyrocketed to a point I don't think it had ever reached before. He was real! As if I still needed proof, HE WAS REAL!

Like the old song says, "His eye is on the sparrow." Faith is a stair step, I have found out. Like a rung on a ladder. David fought Goliath using a slingshot and five smooth stones only after he had fought a bear and a lion under God's anointing. This action on God's behalf, would last forever in my life. "Is anything too hard for the LORD?" (Genesis 18:14).

The Cookout

When we made it to my mom's house, the party left little to be desired. Old friends showed up by the bunches. It seemed like the whole block was there. Family came from near and far. My most surprising visitor was a man who remains my closest friend to this day.

Linwood Taliaferro. We had grown up together. We went from kindergarten all the way through five years of college together. When we were younger we would spend hours on the phone talking about girls, movies, TV shows, sports, you name it.

When we first got out of college, he came to California and stayed in Pasadena for a couple of years. I went back to Pittsburgh. By the time I had moved my family to California, he had moved to Florida, where he found a wife and raised a family. He left them at home when he found out I was being released and came out here to help ensure that my transition from prison to real world be as seamless as possible. His last name, Taliaferro, is the same as my middle name. We got our Social Security cards on the same day, so our numbers are just one number off from one another. He should get a whole chapter, but for right now, suffice it to say that my best friend was there for me.

Another "guest" showed up unannounced: my kids' mom. She made sure to wear her shortest shorts and left no doubt as to what her plans for me were. She told the kids she was there to take back her husband.

My daughter threw the first dagger when she showed her a picture of my new girlfriend.

Her mom responded by asking her to go and get me so that we could talk.

To this point I had only acknowledged her with a dry hi and a kiss on the cheek. I was determined not to be sucked in by fleshly desires. She was sitting on the bed in a back bedroom when I found her, twiddling the photo of Debra between her fingers. "She looks young." That was all she said about that.

She asked me where I was sleeping that night, and I replied, "Right here at my mother's."

She tried to kiss me and I pulled back. The smell of cigarettes was something I had become unaccustomed to. I told her I was concerned about her. I said she needed prayer. Without waiting for an answer, I began to pray for her.

I could tell when I grabbed her hands initially that she was shocked, but she didn't draw away. Here was a woman that I had known intimately for just about twenty years—and I hadn't had sex in around three years—but I was determined that God would get the victory out of this encounter. This would become part of my testimony.

Later, when she was ready to leave, she asked me to take her to wherever she was staying. I looked at Linwood and asked him to ride along with us. I dropped her off and returned to my mom's. I could almost feel the sighs of my mom and auntie. It had been a good day. It had been a great day!

I spent the next week just trying to reacclimate myself to life as a free man. I wasn't actually free. Once you are released on parole, you are still state property. What that means is that your parole officer, PO, can come to wherever you are staying, search your room, and take urine specimens.

I went to the parole office and met my PO. He seemed like a nice enough guy. One of the first things I told him was that I had plans to marry Debbie, someone I had met in prison. I told him she would be getting out in only a few days. I also told him that she was paroling to Corcoran, to her grandparent's home.

Corcoran is a small country town in Central California, about halfway between Bakersfield and Fresno. There's now a large prison there as well, but it hadn't been built back in 1988. Since Debra is writing her own story, I'll just say that prior to her arrest, she had been staying with her son at her grandparent's home. While she was incarcerated, her son, Octavious, stayed with her grandparents. He turned ten shortly after our release.

I haven't mentioned much about my two sons. The thirteen-year-old, Kito, was staying with my mom and was the one who had the most difficulty dealing with me and his mom's situation. The sixteen year old, Rasheed, was actually in a youth camp when I was released. I made arrangements to go to see him as soon as I could.

He had collected a few drug-related charges, mostly regarding sales. The family believed a neighbor had steered him in this direction.

There is still some question in my mind as to whether his mom had anything to do with his activity. I don't think she would have started him on this path, but I had been told that she had either purchased from him or encouraged his drug sales to feed her own addiction. Remembering what I had almost heard on the Chino West yard about her and her unscrupulous activity, I'd hate to think what he may have found out.

When I went to visit him, he was still the same kid I remembered. When he was very young, some older kids convinced him to crawl into someone's house through a doggie door. When the police showed up at our home—his mother and I were still together at the time—we asked them to ride him around the block in an effort to scare him straight.

Evidently this didn't work.

Rasheed had about two to three months to do in the camp before he got out. The plan was for him to come and stay with me at his grandma's.

I had told the family, particularly the kids, about Debra and our plans for the future. They had all seen pictures of her.

I must say that neither my kids nor any family members expected that I would get back with my former wife. Not only did they not think that was best, but neither did her family—the thirteen brothers and sisters who adopted me when we were young. Even her mother felt my leaving her was long overdue.

I'm not trying to put total blame on her. I admit that I played a role. My biggest fault was not knowing my role, since I had never really been raised with a man as the head of the house. It wasn't long after my mother remarried that I went off to school, and only a year or so after my freshman year of college, I was married with my own home.

I will say, however, without hesitation, that she was the major cause of the marriage's failure. She began cheating barely two years into our marriage. She apparently wanted someone older. A manly man, and I was still a boy myself at that time. I had problems, plenty of them, but the disrespect and hardship she put us through was unbelievable.

The marriage would have ended long before if I hadn't held on to some resolve that my kids were not going to grow up without a father. One reason I had moved my young family to California was that I thought such a move would somehow revive the marriage. I didn't realize that even when you change environments, there's a good possibility that that thing causing the disruption on the inside moves with you. Whatever her problem was, it was still there on the left coast, just like it was back in Pennsylvania. Sooner or later she found a way to feed the animal.

I say all that to explain that our divorce brought no remorse to anyone, except maybe her, and I'm not even sure about that.

I contacted the church man who had offered me the job and let him know I was still interested, but needed a little time to get things in order. But I did start going back to that church. The big difference with my church attendance was my sincerity as far as serving the Lord. I had picked up a lot of knowledge concerning the Word while I was incarcerated. Once I got to the state prison, I used every avenue available to me to glean as much about God as I could. The biggest asset was time, and I tried to make sure that my time there was well spent as far as my building a firm relationship with God.

The interference and distractions that are so prevalent in the real world were reduced substantially in prison. They gave us three hots and a cot. We had clothes to wear and no control whatsoever, as far as what was going on outside. It was easy to forget that world and live only in the one you were in.

Naturally, I wouldn't suggest future ministers add a stint in prison as part of their study curriculum, but I can honestly say that the time I spent incarcerated turned out to be time well spent. It was not only justified, but needed. I consider it a divine intervention. There's an aha moment for you.

Even before my arrest, I had prayed that God would take me out of the situation that drug use had caused. I firmly believe that if it weren't for the drugs I would not have put up with the antics of my wife.

My pride and self-esteem had hit bottom even prior to my arrest, what with the financial difficulties, the repossession of a car, the sale of another to a drug dealer for a rock—one-half ounce of cocaine—bottom price, the loss of a home to foreclosure, the loss of a very respectable job I had worked on for many years—a job that had a future that would probably have provided for me and my family well into retirement. I knew what my wife was into, and I knew that others—family and friends—were aware, too. Her nights out turned into days and sometimes weeks before she returned.

Even a quarter of a century later, my heart aches when I think of her disrespect and what others must have thought about me. A wimp, a chump, a punk, all that and then some. Prior to my arrest, I knew of God, but when I walked out those gates thirty-one months and twenty days later, I really knew God, who He was and what He could do.

He was God, and He was prepared to introduce me to the realm of His greatness.

BACK TO NORCO

IVE DAYS AFTER I was released, it was time to go back and pick up the one I had left behind. My daughter and I decided to go back together. I had been talking to Debra on the phone pretty regularly, and we made arrangements. She would come to Pomona to meet my family and then I would get her on a Greyhound Bus so she could get to Corcoran in time to see her PO the following day. Bridgette and I hopped in the car and back to CRC Norco we went. It felt really strange, seeing those gun towers so soon after leaving. We pulled into the parking lot on the women's side, and Bridgette went in to pick up my bride-to-be.

As I waited outside R&R, one of the COs came up to me. "Have I seen you before?"

"You don't look familiar to me," I said.

He continued to make small talk before finally just coming out and asking me if I'd ever been there before.

"Yes, sir."

"How long ago?"

"I was released last week."

"Does your PO know you planned to pick up another inmate?"

I explained that I had indeed told him we were planning to be married soon.

He questioned why the PO would say I could come onto prison grounds.

I didn't know it was against any rules, but I guess ignorance is no defense.

The CO went back into R&R and returned shortly after. "The sergeant says if you don't get your ass off his prison grounds, he'll have you arrested on the spot."

Oh, my. I didn't need that. I asked him to send my daughter back out, since she was driving the escape vehicle...I didn't put it like that.

He went back in, Bridgette came out, and she drove me to a local donut shop. She then went back to pick up Debra.

About a half-hour later, Bridgette was back, but all my attention was on the woman riding shotgun. When Debra got out of the car and walked into the donut shop, I was like a teenager on a first date. I didn't know what to say. I looked into those big eyes of hers and saw the smile that had captured Dan's attention, and my excitement was unbelievable.

Our kiss was the first of many that day.

Linwood, my mother, aunt, and uncles all met us back at Mom's house, trying not to stare too hard. When my uncle finally opened his mouth, he said something to the effect that if he had known there were women like her in prison, he would have gone in a long time ago.

We took tons of pictures, ate something, talked a lot, and kissed a lot. Debra called her grandmother and told her what time to expect her. At first we were going to get the bus straight from Pomona, but we found out she would be better off if we took her into LA. Linwood and I did that. While we waited for the bus, we kissed a lot.

Did I already say that?

LIFE REVIEW

The next time you have a deep need, pray and fast.

To start, you can fast one meal or a half day from all food. While you are fasting, pray to God for peace, for help with your situation, for friends who will influence you for good and protect you from harm, like Dan did for me. Sincerely ask Him to make you a new creation.

3

A NEW CREATION

THEREFORE IF ANY MAN BE IN CHRIST, HE IS A NEW CREATURE: OLD THINGS
ARE PASSED AWAY; BEHOLD, ALL THINGS ARE BECOME NEW.

— 2 CORINTHIANS 5:17

INTERMISSION

'VE REACHED A place in my story where the idea of the *why me* becomes a clearer picture. I look back at some of the things that have gone on since that crucial day in September 1985, and I realize God had a plan.

Most times we see the negative aspects of the *why me*. I'd like to help you see the positive.

So many things could have gone the other way. Being shot could have had repercussions beyond my being arrested and going to jail. I could have been killed. I could have been wounded to the point of losing not only physical capabilities, but mental as well.

What if the clerk had been shot by the store owner? Here in California, that would have been my responsibility and added to my crime.

I know, most people would say I deserved to be shot. Some because of the crime itself, others because I was foolish enough to walk in there with a pellet gun.

Not long after my release, I drove down one of the main streets near my mother's house. As I approached the local liquor store, I saw at least ten squad cars parked along the street and in front of the store. I soon found out that a young man had tried to rob the store and was shot dead. The owners, who had been in the community for years, were distraught. Someone had been killed in their store. To this day, over twenty-five years later, that store has never re-opened. It didn't seem to matter who was right or wrong, although the assumption is that the robber was the instigator.

I easily compared my own situation to that one.

This kid was dead. No second chances, no grace period. I don't know whether he fired his gun first. I don't even know if he had a gun. All I know is that he was dead.

WHY ME?

In a similar situation, I was shot, but somehow given a second chance. What would this kid's parents say about me?

WHY ME?

For whatever reason, God chose to spare me. I like to think that my life was spared not because it was my first real crime—it wasn't—nor because I had prior accomplishments—I blew many of those too.

Was it because my mom and grandmother over the years had prayed over my life long before this situation had happened? I like to think that should be considered—but does this mean this kid had no one praying for him?

I firmly believe that because God is omniscient (all-knowing), omnipresent (all places), and omnipotent (all-powerful), He knew what lay ahead in my life. I think God knew that if He saved this one, He would get a return on His investment.

One thing I have learned to do over the years is to trust God. Trust the decisions He makes. They are His to make. He cannot lie. He does not err. His decisions are final, and I have grown to accept that they are the right decisions.

Yes, we have self-will and that's what separates man from beast, but think about it—only man is out of whack. The rest of God's creations move as He designed them to. When was the last time you saw a dog treat other male dogs as he would a female? Or a horse so dissatisfied with its station in life that it jumps off a cliff?

WHY ME?

Several other things happened after my arrest that could have gone badly for me. The decision that led me to be taken to San Bernardino County Jail instead of Los Angeles County Jail was a huge one in my favor. The jail systems are like night and day, with Los Angeles being night. It is so much bigger. There are so many more gang problems. I'm no wimp, but being in LA County Jail could have had much more dire consequences than going to San Bernardino County Jail.

WHY ME?

Once I was in the hospital jail ward and spilled my guts concerning my law enforcement background, why did my non-secret remain secret? James could easily have told others about the clown he met in the hospital who thought it was such a big deal to be arrested as a former federal cop.

Why did God help him choose to remain silent? James didn't know me from Adam, but somehow he chose not to disclose. He chose to keep my indiscretion or my stupidity quiet, even after I walked into the jail infirmary just days after he did. I would have probably been threatened, beaten, and forced to go into protective custody if word had gotten out.

WHY ME?

Why did God choose to fill me with the Holy Ghost almost immediately after being arrested? Why hadn't I been filled before, when so many others tried to teach or prompt me to speak in a heavenly language? Why didn't I have to wait and tarry like many others that I know?

WHY ME?

For some reason I was given a glimpse of the real jail. I got to spend one night, just one night in J Block. I was given the privilege of seeing just another thing that God had saved me from. I was able to witness how miserable four months in the real jail would have been versus four months in the jail infirmary.

WHY ME?

Lord, why was I sentenced to five years in prison, when the young white boy beside me with twice the crime was given four? Why didn't they find the pellet gun? Why wasn't I given the minimum sentence, which would have been four years, even with the "gun" charge. Could it have been that I wasn't ready to come out after a little more than two years with good time? Would I have been too weak-minded to withstand the temptation of being out there again with my first wife?

What about Debra? If my sentence had been less, I wouldn't have met her. Besides, five years was eight less than the thirteen I could have gotten with the maximum sentence.

What about my own drug use? Would I have lost the desire after only the reduced sentence that I could have gotten?

WHY ME?

What about my dorm and work assignments? God saw to it that I was put in the company of King and Mr. Smith. Convicts indeed they were, but they were also seeking the face of the Lord. The Bible studies and the introductions to other Christian brothers might never have happened. I could have missed out on these very important relationships.

Why was my cast removed after nearly eight months? Just in time for me to get back from federal court and have the opportunity to change jobs. Just in time to apply with Dan at the warehouse and obtain a position that gave me all types of perks and helped in its own small way to build my relationship with Debra.

Speaking of Debra, why me? Why did Dilbert give her letter to me? Why did I write? Why did she write back? Think about our release dates, just five days apart.

For real, God?

Someone tell me God wasn't in this, so I can tell them what a fool they must be. As we used to say, even Ray Charles could see God in this.

WHY ME?

Why did I so insist on stopping at that particular church on the way home? There was one closer, right down the street from my mom. When I saw the doors were locked, why didn't I just move on? Why was I so persistent about getting in and being able to pray? Although I eventually worked there for only a couple of weeks before moving into another more secure position, the offer of a job before I even reached my front doorstep was a booster shot for my faith in God.

WHY ME?

At times, these questions come up daily. I'm sure that as you've read and continue to read you will come across many more. There are many in your life, too.

The world will call these coincidences or mere luck.

Don't be fooled.

God is in control.

WHY NOT YOU?

Take time now to remember the moments in your life that fit together just perfectly to move you into a blessing or out of a curse. Remember each one in your thoughts or write them down as you thank God and praise Him for each.

Whenever you can, tell others the goodness He has done for you. This is your personal testimony; it will encourage others to know that God is real and to seek Him, just as you may have been encouraged to do after reading my testimony.

You might think that there are no times in your life when God has been good. I didn't think so either before I went to jail. And I didn't think so sometimes in jail. But if you ask Him to show you how He has worked in your life, He will. And if you sincerely ask Him to take over your life and restore you life, He will. Then you will see mountains move in your favor because God is a god of second and third and 1,000 chances. You can ask Him right now.

FRIENDS AGAIN

A WEEK HAD GONE by after my release. Linwood returned home to his wife and kids. My best California friend, Harold, took over the "Booker Watch." He told me early on that he had seen the kids' mom hooking on Holt Boulevard in Pomona. He also told me I would need to be careful with her because of the rapid spread of the new disease HIV/AIDS.

Harold and I had met back in 1977, the year I moved my family to California. We stayed at the same apartment complex. We, Harold and his wife Mary, and two other couples who lived in the complex become close friends. One of the couples shared a tropical fish interest, and we also got heavily involved in paint-by-number kits. We all smoked a little weed on the side, but no heavy drinking or drugging. For about a year, it looked as if our move to California had paid off.

Although I worked in Los Angeles, we lived in West Covina, a bedroom community about twenty miles east of LA. However, the kids' mom soon discovered LA after dark and went right back to her old ways. Cocaine use, older male friends, clubs, and staying away from home for long periods of time became her norm. Although I was doing great with the IRS, my home life was deteriorating rapidly. In about six years it began to affect work as I started to use cocaine with my wife.

In the spring of 1978, Harold drew up a petition against the apartment managers, requesting that the swimming pool remain open after 5 p.m. so working people could have use of it. Our signatures were right under his and Mary's on the list. A few days after paying our next month's rent—we even paid it early due to my going back home for my grandmother's funeral—we received an eviction notice. By this time, we didn't have a lease, and I quickly found out that the landlord didn't need a reason to evict us. Harold was devastated because he felt it was his fault. He got me the advice of an attorney friend of his who walked me through the steps that would help us prolong the process as long as possible. However, he told us to prepare to move. It wasn't long before we had found a home. We qualified for a loan and purchased our first house.

After this, Harold and I grew closer. He had a very shady past and had even been given a new identity by the DEA for his help in a drug case. Harold later became an IRS informant under my control, which gave us both a personal and a professional relationship, probably not such a good idea. When I lost my job with the IRS, Harold and I grew even closer. So when I got out of prison, Harold was right there for me. To this day, I have a dollar bill that he gave me when I was released as a token that I would never be broke again.

Harold handled Linwood's passing of the baton excellently. He had worked for the last few years in the chemical dependency recovery field. He almost immediately found me a job working for an associate of his named Sue Sanchez who was getting ready to open a women's rehab within walking distance of my mom's home. Based on just one interview and Harold's referral, she hired me to work security. My job was to spend the night at the facility to ensure that no one broke in and stole the food and equipment she was stocking up for the pending opening. What a blessing. Just a few weeks before I had required security and was in prison. Now, I was providing security for a woman I had just met. Tell me God's not good.

I had worked at the church for only a couple of weeks before this job opened up for me. I explained to the supervisor there that I had a chance to work in a field that seemed fit for a new career. The church had rescued me. Revealing their faith that God can indeed change people, encouraged me to pursue a new life. The recovery center director also firmly believed that people can and do change, but she didn't hold that belief from a spiritual standpoint.

While I was working the security job, Harold tried hard to get me a position where he worked, a much larger drug rehab run by a corporation that had been in business for over ten years. So it was naturally much more stable. They had an admissions position open, and I applied for it. Sue proved to be an excellent referral resource, since she herself had worked for the same employer.

One thing I had learned about Harold a long time ago was that he had a very addictive nature. If it was drugs, he was in with both feet. When he began playing football pools, he put in more research than most professional sports books. When it came to school, he strived to be the best. In fact while I was incarcerated, he had finished his bachelor's degree and was working toward his master's in social work. Once he got the job with this company, Behavioral Health Services or BHS, he moved quickly up the ladder. He was in a management position and was also holding down two part-time jobs as a counselor for other drug rehabs. He had a way of making contacts, and now he was utilizing them for my benefit. It wasn't long before I had an interview. Meanwhile, I continued working at the women's center, which had yet to open.

In mid-July, I was told that BHS was ready to hire me for the position. I talked to my current employer, and she was honest and direct. She stated that during their licensing procedure, if anything came up that would not allow her to hire a recently convicted felon, she would have to let me go. So when I told her about the position at BHS, an organization that she had just left to open her own place, she told me to go for it. She did ask me to continue working for her until she could find a replacement. I agreed, figuring I owed her much more than that. Sue and I would be business acquaintances for years to come.

BHS offered a job that came with job security, benefits, and a very low wage, $6.50 per hour. Would the old former IRS agent have taken a job like this with such a low salary—no. Would the now-humbled, less-prideful Booker, who had not only spent time in prison, but whose first work assignment in the county jail was cleaning toilets, take this job? The same Booker who had been forced to stand naked with a bunch of other inmates while sheriff's deputies, including women, observed us in all our glory?

Yes, I did. God had spent over three years preparing me for this. This was to begin a twenty-five year relationship with a company that was to become home. I would eventually move up and meet extraordinary goals while in their employ, all under the power and will of God.

ROMANCE

MY COURTSHIP WITH Debra had been strange to say the least. Ten months of letter-writing in the CDC, three or four sightings while on the prison grounds, one suspense-filled moment where the romancer risked his freedom by attempting to pick up his girl on the day of her release, and all of this was followed by a day of family greetings.

"I've never been around a family that kisses and hugs so much," said Debra.

Photographs, lunch, and dinner hosted by me, without the candles, champagne and all the other enhancements that generally accomplish a first date. A speedy trip to one of the seedier areas of Los Angeles, which happens to include the Greyhound Bus Station as well as half the city's homeless population. Yeah, this guy really knew how to impress a young lady. By the time Debra boarded the bus for Corcoran, her first thought could easily have been: "What just happened?"

Debra and I talked on the phone almost daily. I got a "high-paying" position at BHS, and Debra found work at a filter factory making all of $4.25 per hour. Yep, we were ready. We decided that December 10 would be our wedding day. How could we go wrong? Our parole officers supported the idea. We would save the state an equivalent of one staff person, since we came at a two-for-one bargain as far as parolees are concerned.

I left it up to Debra to make the wedding plans. She picked red and white as our colors. Perfect for the Christmas season. She began choosing her bridesmaids and I began choosing the groomsmen. The wedding would be held at a church that Debra's uncle pastored in Palm Springs. I asked Harold to be my best man. I asked another close friend, Calvin, from my IRS days, to be a groomsman. My brother, Steven, and Debra's brothers, Marcus and Wayne, made up the rest of the groomsman.

Calvin was another true friend. He was a big part of my IRS story. He stuck with me throughout the process following my dismissal from the government. When I got arrested and was in the county jail he accompanied my mom on one of her first visits. He had the money to bail me out, but I asked him if he would mind giving it to her for expenses and the kids' Christmas. He readily agreed.

It wasn't long before the wedding was right around the corner. Debra had driven down to see me on a couple of occasions. One time she brought her son and her three small sisters. On one of her other trips, we went to Palm Springs where I met her father, mother and brother. He invited us over for a barbecue. When it got dark, I remember standing outside and holding hands with my bride-to-be. I looked up at the sky and hadn't remembered seeing that many stars since my childhood days in Pittsburgh, when my grandmother would point out the constellations.

On another trip, we visited a tent revival at Greater Bethany Church in Los Angeles. Bishop R.W. McMurray was the pastor. We had really looked forward to visiting this church, because we had both listened to his services on the radio while we were incarcerated. His message that evening was "Mr. Big Stuff." I don't recall the Scripture text, but I do remember feeling kind of like Mr. Big Stuff in God's eyes. I was pretty special, I thought.

On this evening I was baptized.

I had been baptized when I was about twelve, but this time I felt like I really had an idea as to what I was doing and what it all meant.

When Debra stayed in Pomona, she would sleep across the street at my aunt and uncle's house. I began the process of trying to find an apartment. I looked all over Pomona, but I wasn't having much success. When the managers found out I had two older boys, they would come up with all kind of excuses as to why we didn't qualify.

I finally found an apartment complex on the border of Pomona and La Verne. It seemed like a really nice neighborhood. I remembered it from my past. I went in and talked to the managers. After running my credit they said no way. They asked about my soon-to-be-bride, but I found out she had an eviction in her history, so her credit was even worse. I prayed and refused to accept no for an answer. I went back and told these people our story. I also gave them a little of their own history, reminding them of the fact that these same apartments had housed some of the biggest crack dealers in Pomona. "If these apartments can change and clean up their image, why would you think two people can't?"

After telling me our family would be on a tight leash and that we would be given an apartment very close to the office, they agreed. We had a place to stay.

We still had work to do as far as the CDC was concerned. I don't know how often inmates get married to each other, but I assume it's a rarity. I had already mentioned my plans to my PO, but the closer we got to the date, I believe the more surprised he was that we were actually going through with it. Debra didn't tell me about any difficulties she had with her own PO. However, there was still this little thing about her moving to Pomona, far away from the county she had paroled to.

CDC approved the move without a hitch.

WEDDING BELLS

WHEN GOD IS behind a thing, it gets done. There are many examples of this in the Bible. In fact, it's full of them. God makes the difficult into not so difficult at all. Naturally a man's faith is the key.

Debra and I had spent many hours praying not only for each other, but about whether or not we were right for each other. We wanted a marriage based on spiritual principles and reminded God of that every chance that we had. Looking back at all the things that had to fall into place, I get nervous writing about it even now. But twenty-five years of marriage shows that it really happened.

However, at the time we were just two fairly new believers who had just enough faith to believe that all things are possible with God. We went through the processes leading up to our marriage as if they were no big deal. We were just another man and woman who wanted to be married God's way. We actually believed that nothing is too hard for our God, and as always, He proved us right.

This was truly a family-sponsored wedding. My aunt and uncle co-signed with a local jeweler so I could get the rings on credit. Some of my cousins and my granddaughter, the flower girl, were in the wedding, and family made sure that they had their gowns. The same goes for Debra's family. My half-brother Steven flew in from Hawaii to be a groomsman. My mom, aunt, and uncle pitched in and purchased a table and chairs for the kitchen. Debra's grandparents gave us a TV. Even my supervisor gave us an old flower-printed couch that he needed to get rid of. Debra's grandfather used his credit to purchase a refrigerator, bunk beds for the boys, and a bedroom set for us. Debra's brother drove to Corcoran to pick up the furniture and deliver it to our new apartment. I don't recall who paid for the photographer, but we had one. Oh yeah, someone brought the cake too. So, thanks to family, we were ready.

It was Wedding Eve. Most of my family had driven to Palm Springs that day, so we all had rooms in a local motel that backed right up to the mountains. The view was spectacular.

On that wintery, desert night, the sky was crystal clear. The stars seemed to jump out at us and the mountains were postcard perfect. I can't honestly recall what the moon looked like. Maybe it had set. What moon would want to be upstaged by the lesser lights of the stars and spoil the wedding of this star-crossed couple?

I took my kids out to dinner. My oldest son was with us; he had been released from the boys' camp a few months earlier. When he first got out, I got him into Pomona High. He was so excited. He brought home his books and had even signed up to play basketball.

However, when his PO found out that he was in a normal school he called the district and had him removed. There was a policy that said if you had a drug-related crime you could only go to an extension school. This broke his spirit, and I truly believe it caused him to have several more years of criminal activity before getting it right. He left home and began staying with a girlfriend whose family members were known drug dealers and users.

I would only get glimpses of him after that. He later explained that because he was gang affiliated, he didn't want rival gang members to come against his two younger brothers. I respected that, but I prayed for a different outcome.

My daughter had moved out of my mom's house with her daughter and soon-to-be husband. So once Debra and I were married, it would just be she, me and two boys: her son, and my youngest.

The kids and I enjoyed our meal. As we were leaving, I thought I had seen a familiar face exiting a taxi. Sure enough, it was my father. This really did my heart good. For a second marriage, I think I had more family support than most. I was ready.

The next day, as the wedding hour approached, I was called and asked to pick up the wedding cake. Harold said he would drive me. The problem was neither of us was familiar with Palm Springs—this was way before navigation systems and Google. Harold gets sort of crazy under pressure, and I'm sure the sight of us in our tuxedos driving around looking for the right Vons grocery store, minutes before the proposed start of the wedding, would have made a good YouTube video. While we were out we happened to pass by Debra's dad, who was still in his construction clothes. Oh my.

Finally we were all at the church. The wedding started about two hours late.

When Debra and her dad made their way down the aisle, she was just beautiful. As she held onto her dad's arm, I realized just how gorgeous she really was.

I think that up until then I had depended totally on God, it was as if she were His selection and I was just along for the ride. God had pulled the strings, manipulated time, and put the pieces of the puzzle together. Until this moment her sheer beauty hadn't dawned on me. Not only had God blessed me with the one I needed spiritually, He had given me a woman who was pleasant to the eyes.

Speaking of eyes, hers were dark and large. They were like two saucers that seemed to reflect all the joy that she had perhaps missed out on as a child. But it was the smile that grabbed me, just as it had caught the attention of Dan at CRC. She couldn't be described without mentioning it. It confirmed to me that she was as happy as I was. The smile was something I could hold on to. The smile told me that she was in this for the long haul, and so was I.

As we stood beside each other, I could feel the flowers she held shaking against my body. My baby was nervous! When we concluded our wedding vows and the pastor presented us to the congregation...

well they say a picture speaks a thousand words, so if I can work my picture into this book, you'll understand. We were officially husband and wife. The two had become one. God had shown up and showed out.

But this was only the beginning.

TWO HEARTS, ONE BEAT

"Whoso findeth a wife findeth a good thing, and obtaineth favour of the Lord." Proverbs 18:22

AFTER THE WEDDING, Debra and I tried to begin our lives as any newlywed couple would. However, we were different from most in many ways and, as most couples find out in the first stages of marriage, we were different from each other most ways. The one controlling factor that helped us to work out our differences was our love for God and His love for us. I wouldn't say he loved us more than He loved others, but we were indeed special.

If I have opportunity to speak to others concerning activating God's love for them, I would tell them that faith is the key. There is an old Christian hymn entitled "Trust and Obey." The words continue as follows: "...for there's no other way, to be happy in Jesus, but to trust and obey."

I once heard a minister compare belief and faith like this. If you ask a man who is starving whether or not a plate of food that you sat in front of him could prevent his starvation and the man says yes—that's belief. But until he activates his belief by eating the food—faith—he will sit there and most likely starve.

An old saying says that "there are no atheists in foxholes." Most people, when put in a life or death situation, will call out to God whether or not they have confessed their belief in Him in the past. The Bible says in the book of Hebrews that you must first believe that He exists and that He can do the things that only God can do. Unfortunately, most of us aren't put in situations where the only recourse is to trust God and Him only. When the Egyptians backed Moses and the children of Israel up against the Red Sea, they had no hope other than to trust God.

There are so many possible interventions for a near crisis that many fail to see a need to call on God. If the cabinets are short of food, we pull out the credit card. If we feel sort of sick, we make our way to a doctor. If a utility is about to be cut off, we find a friend and borrow the money or ask the utility for an extension. There are so many outs in our daily life that we tend to use these options rather than to pray and ask God. Faith is like a muscle in your body. You have to work it out or use it to see some growth.

The main thing Debra and I had in common was our prison background. While in prison, we knew that we had no control over what happened on the outside. When Debra's grandfather was sick unto death, she couldn't seek the advice of some sort of specialist. She told her Christian sisters and I told my Christian brothers to pray, and prayer worked. I don't recall the specifics of his illness, but I later found out that he was diabetic and his hospitalization was related to the diabetes. Even today, during prayer, if the specifics are unknown to me, I always remind myself that God knows all.

I can't say how many times Mr. Smith and I prayed over my divorce paperwork, but we prayed at each step of the way.

Debra and I continued to do this once we were released. We sought God's will concerning our marriage. We didn't just jump into something as important as "until death do ye part" without seeking the face of God.

We even prayed to change the hearts of our new apartment managers. Who initially didn't want to rent to us. They seemed fixed on our inability to change. A few years later, when we gave them our notice that we were moving out of the apartment and into our first home, they admitted how pleasantly surprised they had been during our stay as tenants.

WHAT ABOUT YOU?

What near crisis are you in right now? Have you asked God to provide a solution? How often do you ask Him? God asks us to ask always, like a very persistent woman who won't leave the judge alone until she gets her case resolved. Read all about it in Luke 18:1–8.

Now is the time to pray and don't give up.

WHY THEM?

PRAYER CAN AND will bring out the faithfulness of God. He is a "rewarder of those who diligently seek Him" (Hebrews 11:6).

I sort of left the *"why me?"* behind, as I started to see that God had set the *"why me?"* up for me, Debra, and our children to be successful in spite of all the negativity the world had prepared to throw in our direction.

In some sense people—even family, friends, and saints—would began asking *"why them?"* when it came to the tremendous blessing and story of our life together as husband and wife, mother and father, ex-con and ex-con.

So we now begin this phase. Hold on, as Debra and I frequently told each other, "We are in it for the long haul," and so is God!

When Debra came down to Pomona, she was assigned to the same parole officer as I was. This man really enjoyed the novelty of having two parolees who were married to each other. He quickly assigned us to a vocational rehabilitation counselor who took us under her wing. Since I was working in the substance abuse treatment field, the counselor made a way for me to obtain college tuition, books and supplies, parking, and gas to take classes at a local community college. I needed the certification if I were to continue in that field.

Debra had a long background in cooking and food service, but she had a strong desire to work more professionally as a legal secretary. Once we began taking classes, we continued to work, me in drug treatment and she at a local restaurant as a short order cook. Life was sweet.

In a year, we got notification from the Parole Board concerning our status. Surprisingly, Debra was released, but my parole was extended for at least another year. *Why me, Lord?* my inner voice said.

I was happy for her, but personally I felt more deserving. One evening I was going through one of our drawers looking for some business papers, and I happened to come across her criminal record. It was long and it was violent. *Oh my God.* I actually thought about hiding all the knives and sharp objects in the house. I, on the other hand, had two robbery charges and theft of government property. What was the deal here, anyway? Even though Debra was off parole, the vocational rehab counselor continued to carry her case.

Our church life was a wonderful experience. Debra found a church pastored by a gentleman her grandmother knew. It was a very small church, and we were well received from the moment we entered. They put us to work immediately. I became the Sunday school superintendent, and Debra began studying for her ministerial license. Before long, she was ordained as a minister.

We and the two boys were becoming a normal family, but there were still a few glitches.

WHEELS

T O BEGIN WITH we didn't have a car. The owner of the Volkswagen loaned to us soon needed his car back. It was no great loss, as the transmission had gotten to a point where it wouldn't go beyond second gear.

At the time, we actually thanked God for that car.

Harold had arranged the loan and taught me to drive it, since it was a stick shift and I didn't have a clue. I think it was a 1967 or 1968 VW Bug. It was covered with primer, waiting for someone who could afford to paint it. Once Harold taught me how to drive the thing, I kept it at my mom's home—all of this happened prior to our marriage.

It was in pretty bad shape. You could actually see the street through the rusted-out flooring. Whenever I offered to take my daughter to a local store, she made sure to lean well below the window so none of her friends could see her. She also took me along routes that took twice as long, but were deserted, eliminating most chances of us running into anyone she knew.

The church I was going to at that time was a so-called "name it and claim it" church. I felt so bad driving this jalopy into the church parking lot, that I eventually began parking off church grounds and walking a distance to church. I didn't want people to think I was living in sin and God was punishing me with this piece of car.

It was in fact a blessing, and I should have looked at it that way.

It's funny how what should be looked at as a blessing can actually be seen as a curse, if you're looking through the wrong pair of glasses. We should have rejoiced, because it was either this car, walking, or catching a bus, and anyone who knows Southern California realizes that public transportation is a poor option.

Once Debra and I got married, this was the car we started out with. We had no choice other than to drive it short distances. If we dared to get on the freeway with it, trucks would literally run us off the road, blowing their horns and giving us the finger for driving so slow. It wasn't our fault—the car only went to second gear, and we couldn't go any faster than about twenty miles per hour, if that. So we were a little relieved when it was time to give the car back.

Once we lost the car, we began our version of a family carpool. Pay attention.

My mother had a car that I would borrow in the evening. It stayed at our apartment overnight and the next morning, I would leave the house, pick up my mom and drop her off at the spot where she caught her carpool to work. I would then drive the car to my job in Pomona. I would go home at lunchtime, and Debra would take me back to work. She would then drive the car to her job in La Verne, the next city over. When I got off work, a friend would take me to the restaurant where Debra worked the three-to-eleven-o'clock shift. I would get the keys from her and take the car to the spot where my mother's carpool dropped her off. I would then take mom home, stopping along the way if they needed anything from the store. I would go home and then when Debra got off, I'd pick her up and we'd go home. In the morning the process would start anew.

During February 1989, we began the process of activating our belief and instigating our faith that God would provide a car for us. After days of fasting and prayer, the Lord led Debra to two unlikely sources for a down payment. One was her mom's boyfriend, whom she hardly knew. However, I have grown to learn that she has no problem asking for things. As soon as Debra asked, he told her that he would give her half of whatever amount was in his pocket. It turned out to be several hundred dollars. The next resource came from an even unlikelier place.

God led Debra to ask one of the prison staff who had offered to help once she was released. Debra had already been in touch with the individual, describing the amazing beginning of our story together up to and including our marriage. We were invited to their house and given a sum of money, that when combined with the other, gave us what we hoped would be enough for a decent down payment on our car.

Now here comes the exciting part. We were again led by God to a local car dealer, who offered to finance anyone. When we got there we met a salesman who had us fill out the necessary paperwork. After running our information, the salesman came back with the sad news that we couldn't be financed. We questioned the dealers' advertisement that they could finance anyone. He responded by stating that that didn't include individuals with as poor a credit history, income, and limited job experience as we had.

My wife then stood up in all God's Holy Ghost boldness, right in the middle of the showroom and said very loudly, "Look, mister, God has a car here on this lot for us and you need to go out there and find it!" *Oh, my God.*

The salesman was so shook up he immediately leaped out of his seat and walked away. We didn't know if he was embarrassed, afraid, or just trying to get away.

We just sat there.

A few minutes later, the salesman came back with two sets of car keys. We eventually chose the 1987 Chevy Spectrum. This car was destined to become a big part of our lives for the next eleven years.

It seemed like every few years after that, God would supply us with a new car. Not a car that was new to us, I'm talking a new car. At first it was a Dodge Voyager, brand new, right off the lot. Our income had not increased substantially, but what had increased was our household. Debra had a child, another reason for testimony as she had been told that she couldn't have any more. With three boys, we had to literally carpool to church or other family outings. We would leave one of the older boys at home—whoever's turn it was on that trip—and come back and get them when we reached our destination and trimmed down the number of occupants. We used the same arrangement to get back home unless one of the boys could catch a ride with someone else. With the van God provided we had plenty of room.

Our next vehicle was another van, a Chevrolet Venture. With Debra's real estate business flourishing, we saved our money and a few years later we had enough to buy a brand new Toyota Sequoia. Our income continued to grow and we soon purchased a brand new Cadillac Escalade.

Meanwhile I got to keep that little Chevy Spectrum that God initially blessed us with for a total of eleven years. I was overjoyed—not really. On several occasions I prayed a mixed prayer of thanks and impatience. "Lord I thank you for my car and the fact that it has run so well and efficiently over these last eleven years, but how long Lord, how long?"

God eventually blessed me with a new Honda, and I was a happy camper.

TESTIFY

EBRA AND I became very popular in the church, and it had just about everything to do with our testimony. The Word says "they overcame...by the blood of the lamb and by the word of their testimony" (Revelation 12:11 NKJV). Soon our testimony had spread throughout the Pentecostal Assemblies of the World, the denomination we regularly attended.

Two ex-convicts, former drug addicts, one who was infamous for carrying a shotgun, the other whose life was miraculously spared while being shot during a robbery that he was in the process of committing. Our pastor encouraged us to testify of our past experiences, especially if some of the women were there from the drug rehab across the street—the same one where I had gotten my initial job upon my release.

Good things continued to develop in our lives on a regular basis. In fact, we testified nearly every Sunday. If we visited another church, our experience seemed to have proceeded us, and we were called upon to share our testimony there as well. Many of the members brought their family or others who they knew were having similar problems so they could hear just what God could and would do for his faithful.

It got to the point that a few other church members actually questioned why God had chosen to bless us so. That's where the *why them* came in. They seemed like the older brother in the parable of the prodigal son, who said to his father, "Lo, these many years I have been serving you; I never transgressed your commandment at any time; and yet you never gave me a young goat that I might make merry with my friends. But as soon as this son of yours came, who has devoured your livelihood with harlots, you killed the fatted calf for him" (Luke 15:29–30).

One woman actually stood up in church and testified that she had been saved for many years and wondered why God hadn't blessed her like He was blessing us. She just couldn't comprehend that God would do so much for a couple of "baby" Christians such as us. We had nowhere near the track record she had. Her needs were plenty, and so were her complaints.

Maybe that's why her blessings were so hard to come by.

WHAT ABOUT YOU?

Sometimes people who question God's blessings on others, just don't take the time to see how He has blessed them. Take a moment right now to think of all the good things that have happened in your life: near misses, employments, coincidental meetings, fulfilled needs.

If you haven't thanked God for each of these, you can do it now. It's never too late. It will increase your faith in Him that He is real and will continue to work in your life. This doesn't mean you won't have any more problems, but your faith will move your problems into God's hands and out of your own and produce better solutions, even blessings.

GOD IS ON THE JOB

I N THE SPRING of 1989, our employment took a turn for the better. At the urging of Harold and Paul, a good friend of his, I was promoted to Community Liaison. The CEO Larry Gentile himself, came out and interviewed me, expressing his firm belief that I could do really well marketing the program. He cited my past experiences both professionally and as an addict.

Paul Sharpe became my new supervisor, and we began the process of building a strong private-pay program. I had to familiarize myself with all of BHS' programs, and I became well known throughout the company. BHS was perhaps the largest LA County–contracted provider for these services, so I also became well acquainted with individuals within the hierarchy of the Alcohol and Drug Abuse Program.

Soon after my promotion came a job for Debra. Surprisingly, it was with American Recovery Center as well. She was hired by the Hospital Administrator Jim Elliot, as an Executive Secretary. We were both still in school thanks to our vocational rehab counselor, who like most in her field, took pride in her successes, and we qualified. At this time Debra was taking classes in the field leading to executive secretary. My supervisor knew of her history and how her life had also been changed. He provided a recommendation, as did Debra's current and former employers. Naturally Harold spoke up for her too. Both he and Paul held management positions within the company.

With both of us employees of BHS/American Recovery Center, in a little over a year our income, though still modest, had tripled. God had kept us through the latter half of 1988 on a combined taxable income of a little over $5,000!

I worked a second job for the Red Cross as a telephone solicitor, calling potential blood donors. Although asking people for anything—especially their blood— was not my forte, I had developed an attitude that through God I could do anything, and I was going to do whatever it took to see our lives flourish.

Based on the way things had happened, I firmly believed that God had a strong hold on our marriage, and who was I to deny God? I worked for the Red Cross for approximately a year, maybe not that long. Once Debra was able to go back to work I began to concentrate on school and my full-time job.

During the early 1990s I received another promotion, to Admissions Coordinator, and took over the management of the Admissions Department, as well as the Medical Records, Community Relations, and Communications Departments. I now had about ten or twelve people under my supervision and began reporting directly to the administrator. It would normally not be easy for one man (in this case the administrator) to supervise a husband and wife, but our personalities allowed it to not be a problem for him at all. This promotion led to a significant jump in salary, but God still wasn't through.

The company hired a kitchen supervisor, and based upon his experience in the field, his starting salary was more than mine. I had no idea what his salary was, but Mr. Gentile, without any urging on my part, gave me another raise to keep my salary comparable to the new guy's. It should be noted that this came at the time of a company-wide wage freeze! Even Debra couldn't believe the raise and had the nerve to question—to me only—the fairness of it. Naturally, I had no questions about it at all. I continued to work under the favor of God.

God moved on Debra's behalf too. He indeed works in mysterious ways. Once the wage freeze ended, the administrator opened a position for a human resources person. He advised Debra that he thought this would be a good fit for her and encouraged her to apply. This represented a raise in salary for her, so she applied without a second thought.

After going through the process of applying and interviewing, surprisingly, Debra was not the one selected. On the afternoon that she was informed of the administrator's decision, I saw my dear wife walk swiftly past my office with tears in her eyes. She was headed for the exit. She was trying to rush to the parking lot before the tears really began to flow. She was so distraught at the time that the administrator had to send her home to calm down.

When I got home, we prayed over the situation. We knew it was going to take some doing for Debra emotionally, as she would now be the one to have to train the employee who had been given the position she had applied for.

But God was just beginning to do His work on her behalf. A few months later, Debra was called in early by the Program Director. They needed help in the kitchen. The Dietary Supervisor had been fired on the spot and there was no one to supervise the preparation of the clients' meals. The Program Director knew of Debra's past experience in cooking and asked if she would help out. Debra agreed, and the Program Director was impressed, not only by how quickly Debra was able to get the meals out, but by how she took control of the kitchen staff and client workers. She assisted in the kitchen for less than a couple of weeks before she was offered the job of Food Services Manager. We prayed over it, because Debra had such a strong desire to come out of the kitchen when she came to ARC in the first place. Her desire since our marriage had been to move into an administrative position.

The Lord led her to take the position in the kitchen, which, unbeknownst to her, came with a new salary that was much higher than she was making as the executive secretary. During her period of time in the secretarial field, she had struggled somewhat, because it was all new for her. Once they let her loose in the kitchen it was like she was at home again. Not only that, but she was a senior manager and still reported directly to the administrator.

Debra now had a job doing something that she'd loved ever since her dad had taught her the intricacies of food preparation. She now had her own department, which included several staff and the supervision of client helpers as well. She was the liaison with the ARC dietician and had a major influence on the menu. She was now responsible for the largest budget in the facility.

It was another "God shot" that the money the former Food Services Manager had fought to get not only went to Debra, but as previously mentioned had helped me get a raise as well. So we had both been blessed.

One of the conditions of employment in her new position was that she obtain the same certification the other manager had. No problem with God. Debra was simply directed to go to the vocational rehab counselor and request a curriculum change. The counselor agreed, and as soon as she could, Debra was able to change schools to one of the few in the county that offered culinary courses. Chaffey College also just happened to be a short drive from our job and work.

Debra immediately began to put her mark on ARC's dietary department. Our menus and the quality of food became well known, not only throughout the company, but throughout the county. At every chance they could get, the administrator or the CEO held special events that included food as a central enticement. I would venture to say that there was no other drug treatment program, public or private that fed clients the quality, quantity, and type of food that was served at ARC under Debra's watch. She very much enjoyed teaching staff and client workers. In spite of the quality of food Debra was serving, she was actually able to lower the budget.

As I've stated earlier, Debra did not mind asking, and there wasn't a vendor or food contractor who got by her without giving substantial donations of food in addition to what ARC had to purchase. Attendance at our graduations and special events skyrocketed due mostly to the food. Colonel Sanders I believe, once said, and I paraphrase, that if you give the people a decent meal at a decent price they will come. Debra put this to the test and won time and again. Sometimes she got the whole family involved in budgetary management, such as during Thanksgiving or Christmas. When stores gave out free or discounted turkeys for purchases exceeding a certain amount, the whole Bledsoe family would be in the store, dividing amounts in the shopping carts with food purchases and a free turkey each for ARC.

Debra treated company money as if it came out of her own household budget. I actually felt sorry for some of the salesmen who tried to get around her and actually make a profit. A case in point was a vendor who offered Debra $500 in cash to purchase from them. I assume he was trying to get her to turn a blind eye toward overcharges or product that was not up to par. Debra politely took the $500 and turned it in to the administrator. He was so shocked he didn't know what to do with it. I'm sure he used it to bolster ARC's budget.

When Debra gave this testimony at church, I could see heads shaking again. *Why them?* Who in the world would turn that type of money in to the company? A dedicated saint could and would. A saint named Debra who truly believed that no one could bless her like our Lord and Savior Jesus Christ.

We felt that if something was too shaky to testify about, it wasn't a testimony and didn't bring glory to God. A case in point was a testimony I recall hearing in a church service by a minister. His family was in a financial bind. He was walking down the aisle of a supermarket and clearly saw a twenty-dollar bill drop from a woman's hand. He watched as she kept going. When he got to the spot where the money had fallen, he picked it up, put it in his pocket and politely said, "Thank you Jesus." Really? Wouldn't the real testimony be to have caught up with that lady and placed the twenty-dollar bill back in her hand? I'm sure God would have met the minister's need some other way.

On another note, the position Debra had applied for several months earlier without getting, the one she had wanted so badly, was soon eliminated due to budget concerns. Isn't it amazing how God will save you even from the things you think are His will—things that are actually your will? Even her old executive secretary position was eliminated. God had moved Debra out of the way of disaster, knowing that otherwise our family would have been without the second income she provided.

After a few years, Debra felt the itch to change careers. She had completed her field of study in culinary arts, and that completed her vocational rehab training. She began to study real estate.

"Real a-what?" was probably the response I would have given if asked. I had no idea that was what she wanted to do, and I don't think she did either. But Debra wanted a change, and when Debra put her head to doing something, she usually got it accomplished. So real estate it was. Debra spent less than a year studying and passed the test with flying colors. Her license came about as another miracle that God put together, as she obtained it without too much difficulty. Once again God moved on her behalf. She did all the studying and preparation for the test, and once she felt ready she went to the testing site. She finished the test so quickly she actually scared herself. Within a few weeks the results came in. However, there was a glitch—her criminal record. She soon found out that her license had been held up because her history was under investigation.

After a period of time, Debra telephoned the Department of Real Estate to check on the status of her license. The person she reached on the phone asked her some personal questions concerning her background. Amazingly, in this big state of California, somehow, Debra had been put through to the person who actually had her license application sitting in front of him on his desk.

He concluded his questioning with "Do you believe in God?"

By now, I'm sure you know what she said.

Within a few weeks, Debra had her license and hung it in the office of Century 21 Beachside in Rancho Cucamonga. She had already explained her history to the office manager and to this day, eighteen years later, he and she get along quite well. She is one of the top agents in the office and has received several awards honoring her salesmanship. She frequently receives the Top Producer merit.

I could go on and on concerning her accolades in the real estate industry, but that's her story. For now, I'll just say that she has done extremely well and is as diversified as an agent can be in this day and age. After her first several transactions, Debra put her career in God's hands and resigned from ARC. Her income has far exceeded mine most years and is the reason God has been able to allow us to be the blessing we have been to other churches and saints.

THE MYSTERY OF GOD'S MYSTERIOUSNESS

But as it is written, Eye hath not seen, nor ear heard, neither have entered into the heart of man, the things which God hath prepared for them who love him.
—1 Corinthians 2:9 (KJV)

God works in mysterious ways. It seemed that the sky was the limit for us as far as God's blessing was concerned. Since our release from prison, we had made many new friends and acquaintances. Some of them had no idea concerning our background. One of the doctors once invited the ARC senior staff and their spouses out to dinner. Somehow, the conversation around the table turned toward how each couple had met.

I would have loved to see the expressions on the faces of those around us when we told our story. Unfortunately, we looked at each other, smiled, and decided to pass on that one. Debra, still at ARC at the time, was in the infancy stages of building a real estate business. It seemed that things were better left unsaid. We began to speak less and less about our prison experience, and our backgrounds before that, in front of new acquaintances.

We continued to trust God for just about everything. We may not have talked as much about where He had brought us from, but we were still firm believers of trusting and obeying Him at every turn. I was doing well enough financially, but still making far less than I had been at the IRS before the madness began. So I continued to look periodically for better positions.

One day as I was looking through the want ads I came across a job that seemed perfectly fit for my past experience. They were looking for an accounting type who could put together net worth investigations. These would be used to put a damper on drug dealers who were flocking to Ontario, California, due to the upgraded international airport that had been built. I put my application in and sent my resume in with it.

Now this was the same city of Ontario that had arrested and filed charges against me in 1985. I didn't let that faze me. I believed God to the point of activating my faith in this matter. God could do this. God would do this! I kept telling myself.

Lo and behold, I got a call from the city. It was the Ontario Police Department. Now this sent a chill down my spine. I knew the job was with the city, but I didn't realize it had a direct connection with the police department. I was given a date and time to come in for the interview. On the day of the interview, I must have driven around the block two or three times before I got the courage to go into the station.

Oh, little man, where is thy faith?

When I entered the building, a sergeant at the desk said, "You must be Mr. Bledsoe."

Wow, he knew me by name. Was this a setup?

Right then I started to turn around. I sat down instead, nervously looking through a magazine. A short time later, he told me they were ready for me. He buzzed me through the locked doors.

I went into an office and met the director of personnel, a police captain, and a detective. After introductions, they asked me several questions. I think I did fairly well, but I was more nervous than I had expected. At the end of the interview, they asked me the question that was probably burning in their minds. Did I have anything else that I wanted to expound on?

I did. I went into the details of my past, naturally including my arrest, even though I had put it on the application. We talked for several minutes, but when I left I had a strong feeling that the job was not going to be mine.

They thanked me for coming in and expressed their impression with the fact that my life had changed so positively. I did get the opportunity to give credit for that change to God. They nodded politely and the interview ended. It wasn't long after that that I got the letter in the mail. Thanks but no thanks.

Here is the amazing thing. About two weeks later, I was approached at work by the administrator, Mr. Elliot. He and the CEO Larry Gentile had talked and they felt that I would make an ideal associate administrator. Never mind that this was a totally new position that didn't even have a job description yet, they drew it up for me and me only. That put me right under the administrator, who had the confidence to entrust in me the operation of the facility during his absence. My duties remained basically the same except for occasionally filling in for the administrator. The only caveat was that Debra would report to the BHS Executive Vice President if there were a decision she needed.

This naturally had to have the approval of the Mr. Gentile, who gave me his blessing and would call on me for decisions whenever the opportunity arose. I was able to attend board meetings, and my integrity throughout the company continued to blossom. Not only that, but the new position came with a sizable raise in salary and prepared me for the next step. I had completed my counseling certification several years earlier, but decided I would be better off on the administrative side of my field than as a clinician.

I firmly believe that this job would not have come about without God's divine intervention.

Why did He choose to do so? Perhaps it came about due to the faith I showed in Him concerning the city of Ontario job, which I didn't get by the way.

During the spring of 2005, I received a call from Jim Elliot, the administrator. It was in the early evening, and I was attending one of my youngest son's Little League games. I could barely hear him on my cell phone, but what I did hear was that he had been offered another job and was moving on. He was recommending that the CEO hire me as the administrator of American Recovery Center!

There it was. It wasn't yet final, but I was soon to have made the jump from the least to the most as far as my employment status. As many would say, the rest is history, but actually it's still in the process. God continues to do His thing. My status and pay grade are among the most revered in the company. Mr. Gentile has since retired, and a new CEO has taken his place, but God has proved Himself in a mighty way, allowing me to spend twenty-five years doing a job I truly enjoy. It truly amazes me that God would have people such as Jim Elliot and Lawrence "Larry" Gentile, see the man and woman that Debra and I were and not just two ex-cons!

God will reward your faith, although maybe not the way you expect, but as He wants, and that's even better.

BABY STEPS

URING THE FIRST months of our marriage, Debra had a special request before the Lord. She had been told years earlier that having another child was not likely to happen. Before she got married, this didn't seem to matter. Once we were married we felt that having a child together would solidify our family. Even though we had the two boys, one hers and one mine, our own baby would be a special treat.

Despite the doctor's statement, we both knew God was always in control. So we added a baby to the long list of things we were praying for. Shortly before Debra was hired by BHS, we found out she was pregnant. We were overjoyed.

On February 6, 1990, Josiah Leon Bledsoe was born. He was perfect. His eyes were a blend of grey and blue—skipping back a couple of generations to my great-grandmother, who was white. We wasted little time spoiling him. That goes for my mom and the rest of the family.

Mom had suggested the name Josiah. He was named after the eight-year-old king of Judah. A good king during an era of mostly bad ones. He continued to brag on this into his teens, although we put him in his place by reminding him that his royal linage is spiritual through Jesus Christ and no other.

To say Josiah was spoiled is probably an understatement. Both Debra and I felt that we hadn't done our best with our first kids. We had both put ourselves ahead of them in many ways, in particular our drug use. Although the older kids were never abused and always stayed in the care of capable grandmothers, there was a whole lot more we could have done. Now God had given us a second chance. We always say He is a God of second chances, and this and the rest of our lives together prove it.

When Debra went back to work, Josiah's sister agreed to babysit. He was one of her first clients, and over twenty years later, Bridgette continues to run a very successful day care center.

As he got older, I started to take off work every spring break, taking him to all the places a dad and his boy should go. I'm not a big outdoorsman, but we spent plenty of time at zoos, amusement parks, movies, and playhouses. You name it, and we probably went there. We even rode public transportation just for the novelty of it. We went to nearly every playground in Pomona and the surrounding area. I even went against my own advice and bought him a dog—a Dalmatian and we named him Spotz, to go along with my tropical fish hobby. In addition to all of this, he was a church kid. To this day, I don't think he would know what to do on a Sunday morning if he weren't in church. That's a blessing. In modern day vernacular, Josiah had it going on.

Josiah had a sister and brother old enough to be his parents. In fact, he had a niece and nephew who were both older than he. His addition to the family did not come without consequences. Our 1987 Chevy Spectrum was too small for us all, and our two bedroom apartment suddenly seemed a lot smaller too. But God had another miraculous plan in His back pocket.

Not long after Josiah's birth, my mother retired from her job as a bank teller. She also decided that the three bedroom home she had lived in for fifteen years was too big for just her and my uncle. They decided to move into a seniors' apartment complex. So she offered to give the home to us! We were flabbergasted! The house still had a mortgage, which we would take over, but people just didn't give away their homes. She could have sold the house and made a nice little profit and added it to her nest egg as she went into retirement, but not my mother. She gave it to her only son, his wife, and their upstart family. The payment, even with taxes, was still a benefit over renting an apartment, which we still would have been forced to move out of before long, simply because our family had grown. We not only became home owners, but we had a yard, fruit trees, and everything that went along with it.

Our second child came over eight years later. He was unplanned, but not unloved. Our children were so spread out that I realized a childhood dream, Peter Pan style, of never growing up. How could I, with all of these youngsters around me? I had gone through *Sesame Street* and *The Electric Company* with my first set, *Hey Arnold* with the second set and finally *Spongebob Squarepants* and company with the third, and that doesn't even include the grand- and great-grandchildren.

I've got a lot of growing up still left in me.

WHAT FLAVOR IS YOUR FAVOR?

BISHOP T.D. JAKES and several other pastors often say "favor ain't fair." I don't know who came up with the phrase originally, but I'm sure whole books are written on the subject. When you are in the flow of God's blessing, when it seems that you can seemingly do no wrong, when God seems to turn all the lemons that come your way into lemonade, you get to a point where you feel a need to explain why God has chosen you.

When the *why thems* are coming back to back, you just feel obligated to tell people this is why you feel you deserve this and that. But the best thing to do is to let it alone. You should definitely testify, because this is what God says we should do. "They overcame...by the blood of the lamb and the words of their testimony." However, no further explanation is necessary. Just say, "It's God," and leave it at that.

Favor is not easily explained. Especially as it comes from God. It is a gift from God and, therefore, cannot be earned. It's not like the favor of the world, which can be gained simply by having the right hair color, skin color, body shape, money in the bank, type of car, and so on. God's favor is poured out upon whomever, however, whenever, and wherever He wishes. That is probably why there is so great a controversy around it.

I was talking to a Muslim friend of mine and he told me that the biggest obstacle to him becoming a Christian was that He didn't believe God would select the people of Israel over all the other peoples of the world to be His chosen ones. I can't explain that one, and neither can anyone else I know. Perhaps that's what makes God's favor what it is. It is His to give as He chooses and without trust in Him, you will never accept it.

As you read through this memoir, you too may be questioning God's favor. It's best for the benefactors of His favor to say nothing, other than to testify that it came about. I do believe you can make an effort to position yourself in such a way as to perhaps receive God's favor. Living by the Word of God helps, we suppose, but there's no guarantee.

We can probably all point to a dedicated Christian who seemingly does no wrong, but whose life is a train wreck. Conversely, living contrary to God's Word would not put you in the best position to receive His favor either.

Or would it? What about the guy who robs a liquor store, putting his and others' lives at risk? How does he obtain favor? We see that he did in this book.

The first person mentioned in the Bible to have found favor with God was Abel. God favored Abel's sacrifice and rejected Cain's. It seems Cain spoke the first *whys* as he killed his brother due to the favor Abel received. Cain may have thought, *Why Abel, God, what made his sacrifice so much better than mine?*

We should not allow envy and anger to stir up in us due to another's testimony. God's favor is not always fair. We must accept that. If we live our lives in anticipation of receiving favor, we will be just fine. However, we have to be okay with not receiving it as well. God's favor should not be competitive. It's not something we can control, although the Bible does say, "A good man obtains favor from the LORD" (Proverbs 12:22). Once we get into the details of who a "good man" is, it's easy to see why favor just ain't fair.

We also should note that what may begin as favor may end as something totally different. Or what we thought was an injustice could easily turn into favor. The color of our favor should be clear, that is, transparent. Throughout my saved life I have found that to be true.

In the world, I looked at favor somewhat as Webster defines it: "friendly regard shown especially by a superior...an advantage or benefit." When you think of those things, you think of something you can possibly earn. Now that I have been able to experience the favor of God, I see that I played a very small role in the favor God has shown me. In fact, much of it would not have gone into the book as favor without hindsight, which is the best sight of all. It took looking back and seeing how God used certain situations to turn my life for the better for me to come to the realization that it was favor indeed.

Decide for yourself. Did I receive favor or did I get something that I earned? Could it have been luck? Read on. I have my opinion, and I'm sure you will have yours. Maybe we'll come to an agreement. In the very least you will find things that happened unusual, and that will cause you to ponder. It will cause you to think and hopefully to pass it on. And that's why I wrote this book.

When we made our first home purchase, after being given a home by my mom, we chose Lot 7, since the homes were being newly built. Knowing that the number seven is God's number of perfection, this seemed to be the lot to pick. We were trying to set ourselves up for the favor of God! We loved that home and had two wonderful neighbors on each side of us. We lived there for about eight years, and the home increased significantly in value. We later sold the first home in Pomona, which had also shown a tremendous increase in equity. We used money from both homes to purchase our current home, an estate property. However, the second home, which we rented out, became a thorn in our side and has actually caused a rift between us and a longtime church family. We eventually lost the home to foreclosure. Favor? I don't know. It served a purpose, but we will live with the negativity on our credit for a number of years.

Debra's first home sale came from an unusual source. An older Caucasian woman lived across the street from us in Pomona. She was, I believe, the last of the Caucasians in the area, but had lived there since the tract was built. She was a retired schoolteacher and, like many in the neighborhood, had been watching Debra and I from afar, knowing somewhat of our history. She asked Debra to come over and do a sales presentation. She warned Debra she had a long-time friend who was also a Realtor and was dying to sell the home. If nothing else, she felt this would be good experience for Debra. Schoolteachers! Anyway, to make a long story short, she ended up giving Debra the listing. In a few short months, the house was sold. We had our first sale. We were overjoyed. We blessed God and praised Him for sending a seller and buyers in such a short period of time. Favor?

OUR HOUSE, GOD'S HOME

IN 1995 WE made the difficult decision to change churches. Although we loved our pastor, Elder Harold E. West, we felt our family had outgrown the congregation. Most of the saints were older, and there were just a couple of families who had children anywhere near our children's ages. Our two older boys probably thought they were the only churchgoers in Pomona.

Debra had met another pastor while attending Bible college. He had a church in Rialto, about twenty miles away—not far in California miles. Ironically, the church name was the same, Bethlehem Temple Community Church. We visited the church a few times, and before long announced our intentions to our current pastor. He gave us his blessing along, with a letter of introduction to the new pastor, Michael J. Garrett. Someone who would play a significant role in our lives.

At first I was resistant. We lived in Pomona and worked in Pomona, so why move to a church twenty miles away? Debra, on the other hand, felt that a younger church would not only benefit the boys, but us as well. What did I know? They were both churches that preached the Bible, and besides, I would no longer have the chore of being Sunday school superintendent, a job that was similar to running a mini-church in itself. I loved to teach, but I wasn't overjoyed with supervising the other teachers. When we met with Pastor Garrett, he said he had the perfect job for me: assistant Sunday school superintendent.

Within a year I was the Sunday school superintendent. God has a wonderful sense of humor.

Our new church home was in building-fund mode. The pastor quickly made use of our reputation as far as selling dinners and fundraising was concerned. He was amazed by the amounts of money we were able to donate, just from this activity.

We were faithful tithers. God blessed us in our employment and the church family supported Debra's real estate business. She quickly built a solid foundation of what she calls "raving fans", some of whom remain clients to this day.

GIVING BACK

There are all kinds of sayings regarding the benefits of giving versus those of receiving. We often speak of the relationship between giving and receiving. The Bible says it is better to give than to receive (Acts 20:35). It also says that you will reap what you sow (Galatians 6:7). Simply put, it is a reminder that God pays attention to what and how we give. He loves a "hilarious" giver—an individual who gets great joy out of giving to others or sowing seed into God's kingdom.

> So let each one give as he purposes in his heart, not grudgingly or of necessity; for God loves a cheerful giver. (2 Corinthians 9:7)

Although Debra and I began our relationship on meager grounds, we always took pride in our ability—and, more importantly, our willingness—to give. It wasn't a matter of giving to be seen. The goal was to be seen giving. We have always thought that it is not so much a requirement, but a privilege to be able to give to others in the name of the Lord.

You can't beat God-giving, but it's definitely okay to try. Debra and I have learned to be funnels and not buckets. When God gives us something, whether in word or in deed, we want to be quick to pass it on to others. Let God's blessing flow through you, and watch how the blessings will continue to flow your way.

Over the years, God has blessed us with the ability to give

thousands to the church. We have been audited by the IRS concerning our giving, and even when we proved all but a few dollars, that stickler of an auditor made us pay taxes on the small amount we didn't have documentation for. But that was okay too, because it could have been a testimony to the auditor, that people do have a desire to give large amounts of money to the church.

This is by no means an effort to brag. It is simply a witness that expresses a truism that the more you give back to God, the more He gives you to enable you to keep on giving. It becomes somewhat of a rebound effect. Give, receive, give again, and receive again, and so on. I pray that there are those whom we have given to who will read this book and confirm that we took giving seriously.

Many times God spoke to us and said this person needs that or plant your seed with this individual or ministry. To be honest, many times we wanted to double check to make sure it was God speaking. It's very easy to get caught up in someone's testimony and say that's the one. That's the problem we have to resolve. What family will give us more bang for our buck, so to speak?

It's not all about that, though. We should pray and seek God's direction. Once we get God involved, our giving will be multiplied. Certainly, we want our giving to be well thought of. We want our gift to be used wisely. Many times, people get caught up in how their giving is being used. Did the pastor buy that new car with my money? The First Lady has on a new hat, did we buy that?

Remember that giving is for us. We reap what we sow. We give as unto the Lord, and it's up to Him to decide what it's used for. Our reward is based on our attitude in giving. If we are already questioning what happened to the money, then we've already missed the purpose. Let God get the glory, and He will ensure the best outcome.

Giving is not always about getting some specific thing back in return. In fact, it hardly ever is. God our Father is rich beyond riches. He doesn't need our money, but He will bless you for it. God works through others. I have yet to have God come up to me and just hand me something. It could happen, but that's not how He normally operates. I'm not saying He can't give in that way—He can do whatever, however He wishes—but it hasn't happened with me yet.

I look at it like this. If God allows someone to come up and meet a need I have, there are now two testimonies. Mine and the givers. Not saying that the giver is supposed to go around telling everyone that he gave me something. That's not what I'm talking about. What I'm saying is that now the giver knows to expect something from God. It may come in many forms. It could indeed be a reimbursement of money, but perhaps it will come as a healing. Perhaps that prayer for something he's been praying about is finally answered. However it comes, the giver realizes that God has acknowledged his gift. Thus the second testimony.

Giving is the main area that tries many a saint's faithfulness. If you believe Scripture to the point of giving sacrificially in answer to a request from God, you are truly stepping out in faith.

The Bible tells us to bring all the tithes into the storehouse, "and prove me now herewith, saith the LORD of hosts, if I will not open the windows of heaven and pour you out a blessing, that there shall not be room enough to receive it" (Malachi 3:10 KJV). I'm tempted to say that this Scripture may be used in over 50 percent of Christian churches at one time or another, especially during offering time. Many of us get hung up on this. We look for all types of reasons to bypass this verse.

There have been so many times I have felt I just couldn't afford to tithe. But as one minister put it, if you reach this point, you can't afford not to. I've included this portion in my story not because I'm on a tithing bandwagon. Nor do I want to get into a debate concerning tithing or giving in general. The point I want to get across is that I feel so much better when I am able to give to the Lord.

In our early days of salvation, we did a lot of fundraising activity (mostly cooking) to raise money for the church. Debra even made baskets, and I offered to do tax returns with all proceeds going to the church. God had blessed us so much that we just wanted to do whatever we could to give back to the Lord. But there is one area we have struggled in and still do: the giving of our time. I pray that we are able to reach a point where our time becomes as easy to part with as our money. There are others who may not have the money, but have the time, so I guess it all balances out in the kingdom.

Giving. It is such excellent proof that you believe God and trust His word. We don't keep our eyes on a pastor or an organization that we happen to be giving to. We keep our eyes on Jesus, and He takes care of the rest.

It is indeed a major test of faith and it is faith that keeps us. It is our faith that we have to rely on. Our faith will ensure our salvation. Our faith will be the vessel that we are able to pass on to others. Hopefully, they in turn will pass it on to others, and we will be vessels for the use of our Lord.

Just recently our church announced a "Day of Giving." This was not new to us, but with everything requiring giving, it just seemed to sneak up on us at an inopportune time. I was on disability from the job and the real estate business was still in a downturn. Debra went to Bible study the Tuesday before and was excited about what goes on when we give.

Sometimes we have to be reminded about what God has done for us in the past. There have been times I actually forget about my testimony until I find myself giving it again to someone during a conversation. Then it dawns on me that God actually did that for us. Wow! Isn't He great?

We may have gotten to a point where we were forgetting what God had done for us in the past, based upon our giving. It's funny because all we have to do is look around at the home, vehicles, furnishings, and our health and that should be encouragement enough, but we're human and we sometimes sit right in the middle of our blessing and forget who gave it to us and why.

When Debra came home from the Bible study, she was as excited as she used to be when we cooked the barbecue dinners to raise money. "Honey, God just laid it on my heart to do something special for the Lord on this Day of Giving."

I looked at her, knowing our bank accounts didn't hold anything "special." I looked at the glow in her face. She also knew our present situation, but it wasn't our situation that she wanted to dwell on, it was the feeling of a need to give back to God. "Okay, what's the plan?" I asked.

Out came the pots and pans. She needed to say nothing more.

WHY NOT YOU?

What can God do through you? What gifts, talents, skills do you have that will help others? If you're not sure who you can help, ask God to bring someone into your path who can help you. He will certainly do it. It's time to see how God works through people to bless people. Just ask.

CAN GOD CALL A TIME-OUT?

WHEN WE WERE kids playing various games (Tag You're It comes to mind) we frequently found ourselves calling time-out to allow our beating hearts to catch up with our legs, or to enable us to escape from the impending doom of being the next one to be "it." Even in our adult games, time-out becomes a frequently used tactic to catch our breath or to re-strategize our next move. Time-outs allow us to gather ourselves, analyze, and perhaps move in another direction. Time-outs have become very popular in raising children, supposedly giving them an opportunity to re-think their last move (or their next one).

I'm sure that we have all had occasion to wonder whether God had called a time-out in response to one of our petitions. Think about it. God can do anything but fail. However, fortunately for us, time is not in God's nature. He is omnipresent through all space and time. He is unchanging and cannot lie. For that reason, His Word is Truth.

But where does He go during those periods when we seem to need him tremendously and just can't reach Him? We have to realize that He is always there, but what we consider time is just not on His schedule. It's common for us to say He is always on time, and that encourages us to wait on Him.

God allows us to go through our lives, adjusting, re-adjusting, and situating ourselves to reach heaven. So in essence what we think as

God's time-out is actually ours. His goal is for us to take as many with us into eternal life as possible. We are to be witnesses to all corners of the earth, testifying to anyone and everyone through words and deeds that will aid them in their journey. The Williams Brothers recorded a song that says: "I'm just a nobody trying to tell everybody, about somebody, who can save anybody,...telling the people about Jesus." That's our ultimate goal. The "nobody" part ensures that we are giving credit to whom credit is due—God. As we do this and they in turn do this, the kingdom expands. Remember that the spreading of the gospel basically began with the twelve who turned the world upside down, pointing to Jesus as the Way, the Truth, and the Life.

My wife has a saying. Whenever I ask her how she got something done or where did something come from, often her response is, "While you were sleeping." God not only can't take time-out, but is working things out while we are sleeping. Many times our sleep is not the natural sleep we often think of, but our sleep is the periods of doubt and unbelief that all honest Christians will admit have come upon them at one time or another.

In the Bible we read about a man whose son was possessed by demons that the disciples could not cast out. His response to Jesus regarding his belief was "Lord I believe, but help thou mine unbelief" (Mark 9:24 KJV). In other words, he wanted to believe, but acknowledged that he had doubt. Doubt in turn darkens faith, and Jesus had difficulty operating in situations where there was little or no faith.

WHAT ABOUT YOU?

Do you doubt? Do you have little faith that God can work things out on your behalf? Do you feel like everything good that happens is only because of your efforts? If so, it will be difficult for you to receive what God can do for you. God wants to get the glory for what He does your life. Your testimony about what He does for you and with you, like my testimony, will bring people into deeper faith and blessing. There is no doubt that God is real. Sincerely ask Him to show up in your life and He will.

SEEING BLESSINGS IN THE STRUGGLES

Being blessed by God does not mean we have not had struggles, disappointments, physical ailments, or sadness in our lives. Debra and I have had to suffer through many pitfalls since we began our lives together. Sometimes we suffer well, at other times not so well. When we suffer well, God immediately gets the glory. When we struggle, it's up to us to go back and praise Him, in retrospect, as we realize that we actually had the victory all along.

One evening, during a time when we were struggling financially and I was working two jobs to help make ends meet, I was served with documents regarding a school loan that hadn't been paid. I knew I owed the money, but they couldn't or wouldn't make arrangements that would make it easier for me to meet the debt. The loan was nearly twenty years old at the time, and I had actually forgotten about it. But that's no excuse; the money was owed.

When they decided to garnish my paycheck, this really put us in a tight spot. I went to court in an effort to turn things my way. I prayed and fasted before the court date and kept telling myself that in spite of all the circumstances against me, including the high-powered attorney who kept sending me the threatening letters, it was going to be me and God going before that judge. I stood before that judge and answered one question, "Do you owe the money?"

The judge pronounced in favor of the plaintiffs. I was devastated. I had prepared a long statement that I never had the opportunity to read. I felt all alone. Where was God? Had He called time-out to discuss something with me and I failed to hear it? No, He was working things out in another way. A way that allowed my testimony to be even greater! A way that allowed not only the garnishment to be removed, but took care of the entire loan.

On the day before our youngest son, Joel, was born, Debra's grandfather passed. This started a chain reaction in which Debra lost not just him, but her grandmother and her father all within a matter of months. Three of her biggest supporters, if not the greatest supporters (excluding me and God) were taken seemingly all at once. I saw my wife's heart break time and again during those five or six months as the phone calls came in so unexpectedly. Both her grandmother and father were taken suddenly, without warning. We attended the funerals with our heads held up, believing that they had lived lives according to God's will and that we would see them again in heaven.

At about the age of ten, Joel was discovered to have Crohn's disease. He still has it. I say that because many times we go through life as Christians tending not to speak of the negative until it becomes positive. However, God told His people during the fall of Jericho that they didn't have to wait until the battle was over, they could shout now. I can honestly say that, based upon the faith-building experiences I have had throughout my life, God will work through Joel's medical condition as well. It hasn't happened yet, and may not happen during my lifetime or according to our expectations, but just knowing He is able is enough to carry me through. I may be sleep. I may be on time-out, but God's nature is so much greater than me. That's why He's God!

On March 30, 2005, we received a telephone call from my mom. She spoke of having congestion and stated that maybe she should go to the emergency room. First, though, she wanted to hold off. We prayed. When she called back a few hours later, still feeling bad, I said it was time to go. She lived within minutes of our home, so I drove to pick her up. When I picked her up, I asked her if it was congestion or chest pain, thinking I should call 911 if it were the latter.

She insisted it was congestion.

We got into my car and headed toward the ER, listening to J. Vernon McGee, the preacher whose sermons continue on the radio long after his death. We both liked him and discussed his ministry as we made our way to the hospital.

When we arrived, we went in and I waited while they did their initial intake. I parked the car and got back as the triage concluded with an RN. We were sent to a waiting room.

We talked about everything imaginable. She had gone to a couple of funerals during the past couple of weeks, and we discussed those people as well. As you know, I loved my mom, and these types of conversations came frequently, although most times over the phone. In fact, when I first moved to California, mom would call every morning and hang up after the phone rang once. It was her way of letting me know she was okay back there in Pittsburgh. She followed my little family to California after my grandmother passed. Once she got out here, she was both mother and grandmother and loved her role.

Before I even realized it, we had been sitting there for nearly two hours. Mom asked if I thought she was close to being seen.

I looked around and saw a few people who had been there when we arrived. "We probably have a little bit more of a wait."

She said she was going to go to the restroom.

I found out where that was and told her that if she got lost on her way back to just show staff her wristband, and they would direct her back to the waiting room.

When mom came back and sat down she said maybe she shouldn't have gotten up, because now she was really feeling bad. She had gotten pale and began gasping for air.

She fell over on me, and I hollered for assistance.

Other patients began to yell too, attempting to get the attention of the nurse behind the glass window.

Finally she rushed out and assessed the scene. She went back to a phone and called "Code Blue." She came back and told me to lower mom to the floor. As I did so, mom gasped what seemed to be her last breath.

An attendant came with a gurney and immediately carted her away. I called my wife, in tears. "Come quickly. Things don't look good."

We buried my mom just a few days before my fifty-fourth birthday. As I sat during the funeral listening to the comments and words of respect, I observed her many friends and family. Mostly, I looked at the grandchildren and great-grandchildren God had blessed her to share with her one and only son. The one she still called Butch, who had taken on so many of her traits.

I thanked God. He had taken her quickly. Mom had not suffered. He had allowed us to have one last lengthy conversation. He arranged it so she died in my arms.

One of her cousins later told me that there was no other way my mother would have preferred to go. Most importantly, Mom was saved and had lived to see me also make a comeback, accepting Christ and teaching the good news of the gospel. God was there all along. I knew I would see her again in our spiritual eternal life in heaven.

We need to remember that God is indeed in control. He knew exactly when we were going to experience death or illness. He knows when things are going to go awry on the job. He knows when members of the family may act up. When you live life for Him, He is the Conductor. He orchestrates the good and the bad. He doesn't need time-outs, and neither should we.

We have to trust and obey. We have to lay our faith on the line.

WHAT ABOUT YOU?

What struggle are you going through? You can ask God to conduct the situation for you. You can ask Him to lead you on the same path that He is on so that together even the difficulties of life will produce blessings and everyone will see the great things God has done.

FAITH

"Faith sees the invisible, believes the incredible and receives the impossible." - Anon

IN THE MOVIE *Indiana Jones and the Last Crusade*, Indy must cross a huge chasm inside a cave. His father whispers, "You must believe, boy." Indy realizes it requires a leap of faith. He closes his eyes, then steps out into nothing. His foot lands on solid stone—a bridge to the other side. The way is narrow, and an optical illusion hides it from sight, but step by step, he makes his way to the other side. Stepping out in faith! With each step he took, the next became easier, until finally he is no longer walking but actually running through those final steps.

There are many examples of leaps of faith in the Bible. Those examples are there for our use. It's not easy to step out on nothing, but after trying it a couple of times it's not as hard. Think back. Have you gone through challenges in your life that required you to become an Indiana Jones? If you've gone through more than one—and if you think long and hard enough, you have—then you also have to admit that the next time was easier than the first and the next and the next...

I've always been under the opinion that it is easier for someone who is poor to display faith in God than it is for a wealthy person. Jesus gave an example of the rich young ruler in Matthew 19. After being told to sell all he had, he walked away sad. His commitment was going to cost him a lot, and he knew it. We don't hear that he ever came back, so all I can do is assume that the sacrifice was too great. That's why I feel poorer people—I count myself among this group—tend to believe God more readily. We have less risk. We also have greater needs.

Please don't get me wrong. I'm not saying that no wealthy person will make it into heaven, and God forbid if I were to say that all poor people will make it in. I'm just saying it's easier for the one and more difficult for the other. I'm sure there are many differences of opinion out there, but that's mine.

I love to see doctors, lawyers, and other rich professionals put their trust in God—I now put myself in this group as well. You would think they have all they need and, perhaps, according to worldly standards they do. But something is missing. It's that void they are trying to fill. You see, they have tried it all, or have had the ability to, but at some point they come to realize that only God can bring peace.

When I made my bed in worldly ways, smoking weed and drinking liquor, I'd always tell people that what I really wanted was peace of mind. There are many things in this world that can and will bring temporary peace, but lasting peace of mind can only come through having faith in God. Rich or poor, it doesn't matter.

As saints of God, we are all believing Him for something. In the spiritual realm our spirits should line up with His and our desires should line up, too. Again, it's our faith that activates our belief.

WHAT ABOUT YOU?

Throughout this book, you have seen examples of our stepping out in faith. My hope is that the results that have come to Debra and I will cause you to step out on faith as well. We're not special—you can do it too.. My desire is for you to take those steps of faith that God has laid before you to reach the ultimate relationship with Him.

What step of faith is He asking you to take?

When will you take it?

A REAL MAN: REAPING THE CONSEQUENCES

IT IS IMPORTANT to bring up the great influence a dad has on steering a boy's life down the tracks or up the tracks. My Dad was definitely a man's man. He didn't take much from anyone. He had played football and was proud of me and my brother who followed in his footsteps. He was a cop for the Cleveland Police Department, and there's something about cops and their demand for respect. I saw it during my time in law enforcement with the IRS, but not as much as with local police officers. He later became a bodyguard for Don King, the fight promoter, and that allowed his ego to continue to rise to even greater heights. He had command of his household. What he said usually went, although my step-mom would speak up on things she felt passionately about.

At home, my dad pretty much avoided arguments with my stepmother, and I don't recall any of us getting spankings. I had two younger brothers. I also never saw him hit or threaten my stepmom. He did speak with a commanding voice. A voice that was fearless and demanded attention. Knowing the stately woman that his mom was, my grandmother, and her command for all of us to treat women like ladies, my dad got his respect for women honestly.

He saw the problems I had with my first wife. He consistently told me, "It don't take two mules to pull a cart, especially when one is kicking the other in the behind." I knew what he meant, but I had also made a commitment not to leave my children as I felt he had abandoned me and my mother.

This was the background I relied on once I started having children. Fortunately, my first was a girl and she was born to be spoiled. The last five, from ages forty-three to age seventeen, are all boys, and that's where the challenge comes. Not only with the children, but with the first wife.

I have to admit that in my first marriage, I didn't have a clue as to how to be a husband. This was the primary area not covered by the "peek-a-boo" training I got from the men I looked up to. My training hadn't covered those duties of a husband that went on beyond a child's eyes. I got the how to have babies part right, but other than that I failed in that first marriage. Due to my inexperience, my first wife, a kid herself, was easy pickings for the older men she sought out.

In raising my first set of children, I probably did most things wrong. I loved them and always thought to put them first, but I didn't spend much time teaching the boys about what life had in store for them. I was a poor example too. This was the early '70s, and I was in college for those beginning years. Not only was I away from home in Philadelphia, but when I was at home, I also carried the bad habits of smoking weed and drinking beer in front of them. They became part of the gang.

I set a further bad example by putting up with all of their mother's antics, afraid she would leave and take the kids as she often threatened to do. I spoke about my strong desire to be there for my kids, and my first wife took advantage of her power. It became her favorite weapon, throughout nearly all the years of our marriage. Ironically, in my effort to hold on to them, I was eventually forcibly taken from them as I spent nearly three years in the state penitentiary.

It also didn't help that I allowed their mom to treat us all as if we were four weights anchored to her neck, disrupting the life she had set for herself. Oh sure, I was a nice dad, a good man, and I had completed college on time in spite of having two children (the third was born after I graduated) and an unfaithful wife.

By the time I finished college, I had secured a great government job, a job with tremendous promise and potential and we should have been on our way up.

But down we headed, even after I made a decision to move them all to California, 2,500 miles from home, thinking a change in scenery would somehow help our condition.

The one thing I didn't do, that I should have done very early in marriage, was to stand up and be a man. To put my foot down, as they say. I didn't know how to do that. I was a man on the football field, I had become a man growing up in the hood. But I wasn't a man in my own household.

Most of my household training was given to me by the older women in my life, my mom and my grandmothers. I had learned early to treat a woman with dignity and respect. Unfortunately, my first wife took that as a Get Out of Jail Free Card and played her pity-me hand throughout most of our marriage. My strength did nothing for me and the kids, because it was misplaced.

I longed for a victory that would not come until I received Christ into my life. I couldn't become the man God had created me to be, because I had no idea who that man was and where I could find him. My true purpose didn't come until much later. Too late, probably, for that first family of mine, but not too late for my second wife and the second set of children. I had to leave my past and pick up on what God had given me.

It was my time. It was God's time.

It was time to put aside the foolish things and to pick up that order God had entrusted to the leader of the home. Fortunately, I did get a chance to sit down with my older children and explain to them how I thought it had gone wrong. I took each of them separately to a meal and we sat down and had a heart to heart talk. I hope it helped them. I know it helped me just to be able to get the burden off me. It has been nearly twenty-five years since those talks, and the talks have been backed up by my walk. I believe they understand, not that they blamed me outwardly, but I'm sure my daughter felt I should have rescued her and her brothers from the insanity, simply by taking them all and leaving the madness long before I did.

My story is not unlike others who grew up as I did. Unfortunately, I think it's getting worse. The last time I looked, divorces are not declining. Arrests and subsequent imprisonments are not declining either. Absentee fathers are well on the way to record-setting numbers.

A family without a father sets off chain reactions throughout neighborhoods, cities, and our country. We are looking at a society that is well on its way to proving the importance of God's order. The father-husband figure is dwindling, and the repercussions will be tremendous. Satan has his eye on the cornerstone of the family, the dad. As a society we must work toward resolving this issue.

Since saying "I do" for the second time to my present wife nearly twenty-five years ago, I have learned a lot about being a husband, father, and man. Most of the change came about due to my salvation. Accepting Christ as Lord and making every effort to live a godly life has made all the difference in the world. I have read and studied hundreds of Bible verses that address my responsibility not only to my family, but to the church and community.

As a saved man, my acquaintances and friendships naturally changed. I no longer drink or use, and that's a big deal. The experience of three years of incarceration left an indelible impression upon me. I looked at the men I was surrounded by and realized that but for God there would be no difference.

Am I saying men are inherently evil? Yes, I guess I am, ever since Adam.

But God.

I don't think prison was the changing influence in my life. No, prison was the intervention God used to get my attention. Thank God that not everyone needs so drastic an intervention. Prison gave God the opportunity to sit me down and speak to me. He spoke through various channels: Bible studies, radio ministries, prison ministries, other convicts, my mom, and of course my wife.

Since the joint is where I found Debra, it was indeed a major tool that God used to bring us together. All the miraculous things that have happened since then would not have happened between she and I if it were not for the chain of events that began while we were incarcerated.

All the worldly stuff that tends to hinder our communication with God was pretty much removed while I was "away," as my mom used to call it. I had the opportunity to listen and speak to Him. I was able to reflect on all the mistakes I had made. Certainly, it wasn't completely my fault that I lacked the understanding of what should be expected of a man. But the tools God gave me—mostly His Word—went a long way toward helping me overcome the shortage of knowledge that I started out with.

Thanks to my mom and grandmothers, I knew to treat women with respect. They were the ones who instilled in me the manners I still carry to this day. Opening the car door, allowing them to enter and exit doors first, giving up my seat rather than make them stand in crowded spaces—all came from them. Their teaching and upbringing helped me tremendously. It came from a women's viewpoint and was slanted in favor of the woman. This was the opened door that my first wife took advantage of. That in part was why she got away with so much evildoing. I still should have stood like a man and took the reins of my responsibility. I didn't, and she took my kindness for weakness. It worked for her, but destroyed our family.

The verdict is still out on the impact on that first set of children. They are adults now, and I haven't seen the results of my lack of experience in many areas of manhood. I suppose it would affect the boys more than my daughter. It would be hard to believe that all their viewpoints weren't changed in some way. My two older sons have had their share of problems with the law, so that's not a good sign.

A strong man at the head goes a long way toward building a strong family, and strong families build strong communities. I failed in a lot of ways. Oh sure, I was looked at as a great guy. A great catch for any woman who deserved a dedicated husband and father for their children, but I was a failure when it came to raising boys into men with strength.

In his book *Bringing Up Boys*, Dr. James Dobson speaks about how even our society today tends to downplay the role of the traditional male. It is one of those books that you read and think *now you tell me*. I recommend this book and another by Myles Munroe titled *Understanding the Purpose and Power of Men*. Both of these books have given me great insight on the plight of boys and men in today's world. I am sure that there are many other books that expound on the priorities and pitfalls of being a man. If you are a man reading this, grab one of those, written by an expert on the subject. It will do you good.

Did a fatherless home have an effect on how I turned out as a man? It definitely did. My mom did a wonderful job, don't get me wrong. I've bared my mistakes in this writing, and I don't think I turned out that bad. But is that like a mass murderer saying, "I just had one bad day"? I don't think so, but everyone is entitled to their opinion. Based upon my personality and general attitude, I would say I'm a pretty good guy, but sometimes being a "good guy" doesn't cut it. If I had spent more time around a father figure, one who was a positive role model, I could have gleaned strength that would have made me well rounded. I would have had more positive traits to pass on to the young men I have raised.

God has blessed me to be the father of five young men and one woman. He's given me eleven grandchildren and seven great-grandchildren. Over the last twenty-five years, I have passed on good information to the men as far as their manhood and responsibilities to their families, the church and the community. That can't erase my prior years' improprieties, but it's a start. A start that I pray will carry on into the future generations of Bledsoes.

I now choose to be meek. Jesus showed meekness as a quiet strength, and that's okay. Debra says I'm an appeaser, and I can't disagree with that assessment. I have to admit that characteristic alone has caused much of my life to be as it is. I'm comfortable though. I'm comfortable in my own skin, and I've had opportunity to pass this on to my daughter, sons, and grandchildren.

The younger ones don't know my history and will be shocked when they find out, but it won't be hidden from them. I want everyone—them in particular—to see that a man can change. With God that change is a great one. A definite change for the better. A change that has given me the opportunity for eternal life and not eternal damnation. A change that can be passed on to others, to give them hope for themselves, family members, or friends. It is a testimony to the glory of God and will help other Christians see their way through difficult and trying circumstances.

HAPPILY EVER AFTER?

I S THERE SUCH a thing as happily ever after? Well in my mind, if you are writing your own story that would be a difficult sell. Unless you could write it from heaven, how would we know? The happily ever after's that we are most familiar with are fictional stories written by another to summarize the life of someone who has passed on.

As I conclude, I would say God has given Debra and I a good life. It hasn't been a life without challenges, but where is the victory without challenge?

Are there things I would change? Well, all good Monday night quarterbacks would change something. I know I could have done things differently at times. Our family relationships are not where they could or should be, but what family is perfect?

When you have a second marriage, wherein both prior marriages included children, trouble is almost a given. The fairy-tale world of *Eight is Enough* even included an episode or two that pointed out the divisions that can come about when you try to combine stepchildren, inlaws, and so on. You are bound to run into trouble.

Most of our troublesome circumstances have come on account of my former marriage. Although Debra had a child prior to our marriage, he was fairly young and his dad has made little or no effort to be part of his life. However, even that could have caused problems for our son.

My hat goes off to my wife, who only recently reminded me that she was just twenty-eight years old when we married and it just happens that the man she chose to marry not only had children, but grandchildren as well. (Before you snicker, I am not that old, but grandchildren came to me at a young age, the first when I was just thirty-three years old). My wife spoke of the fact that she not only had to learn to be a wife and mom to a ready-made family, but a grandmother too. Oh, did I mention that she was an ex-con, experiencing all the stereotypes that come along with that designation as well?

I was raised as a family guy even without my dad, because that's how my maternal grandparents and paternal grandmother did things. In fact, my paternal grandmother had a rule that pretty much said once a family member, always a family member. It was that philosophy that allowed room for my mother and I on my dad's side of the family even though she and my dad divorced before I could walk.

Debra, on the other hand, came from a home that included both parents, but did not include the same family background. When she and I first married, I had family traditions that I struggled to hold on to, such as the family gathering together on Christmas Eve to exchange gifts. Debra wanted to build new family traditions, which I struggled to grasp. How did this unlikely couple become a pair? God and only God!

As far as our career paths have gone, Debra is definitely the one who has shown the courage to jump into uncharted waters with both feet. Her career has gone from cook to chef, to minister, to administrative assistant, to Realtor, to sales (you name it and she'll put a price tag on it), to journalist, to esthetician, to franchise day spa owner, to...

I honestly don't believe it will stop there. God has blessed her to seek life and pursue it. I love what God has done for her, and it encourages me on a daily basis. I marvel as she conducts her more mundane duties of being a housewife. As I watch her cut up a chicken and prepare tonight's dinner I wonder, *"How could a woman with so many talents fry chicken that tastes this good for her husband and two boys?"*

On the other hand, I have managed to stay satisfied with what life has given me. I've had two real employers in my whole adult life (excluding the one-month stint as a security guard when I was first released from prison, and the short period of time I worked part time with the Red Cross). My job with the IRS was extremely successful, right up to the point that they took my badge and gun for allowing money to disappear from an undercover checking account. Prior to that, I had moved up the ranks so fast that many of my peers questioned what I was going to do at age thirty-five, when I still had twenty years of government service still left before retirement.

One black agent had told me I was able to move up so quickly early in my career because I was a "nonthreatening black" to my superiors and counterparts. I guess I fit the bill. He predicted I would go far fast, and he was right. At least right up until the moment cocaine interfered.

I jokingly tell people now that at the time I didn't have a problem with the cocaine, but the IRS sure did. Debra calls it being an "appeaser," and she's right on target. I was the teddy bear of law enforcement. I worked hard, but for whom? I don't know if I ever really liked the job, but I have a lot of stories to tell. That's for the next book.

Happily ever after?

I began to experience back pain after a job transfer put me on the freeways of Southern California for five hours a day. When I could no longer take the drive, I opted to stay home and filed for disability. Things were not going my way, but God always has a plan for His way. The writing of this memoir began when that job ended. My wife, ever the encourager, told me this was a good time and place to start. So I did.

The past nearly twenty-five years have been happy ones for me. Not that the first thirty-five years were all that bad, but as you've seen, I've made poor choices and paid for them. The difference is that the last twenty-five years have come with hope. The hope of being able to see the ever after in a positive light.

As I conclude my story, which is basically the story of Booker's midlife, I have to admit that, as with everyone else I know, *why me* has been a big question throughout my life. I have enjoyed writing this memoir, and I will enjoy talking about it even more. My prayer is to have an opportunity to sit with people of all nationalities in an effort to explain God's goodness in my life.

Happily ever after?

I hope so, but for right now I can say unequivocally "happily." The ever after is to be determined, but I am headed in the right direction. My destination is heaven, and there happily ever after is a given.

I hope these few words concerning my present outlook on life will help those who are struggling with life as Christians to put at ease a battle they are destined to win, should they live as faithful followers of Christ. I also hope this book will somehow reach others who may not have given God a chance to be real in their lives.

Looking back at things, I can see the *why me* in all of its glory, both good and bad. I've learned to accept the *why me* as *why not?*

I'm moving on from here.

What about you?

LIFE REVIEW

WHEREVER YOU ARE in your life journey, you have a choice to make. You can choose to seek God or you can choose to seek evil. The choice you make will become the story that people will read of your life—it will be your testimony to your children, parents, friends, and the world. It will either tell them how great you are or how great God is through you.

Your testimony starts now.

It starts with sincerely asking God to take over your life and make you a new creation. You can do that now.

It goes on with finding people who will influence you for good not for evil. Who can you start hanging out with that will be good company in your life?

It continues with you giving back to others what God has given to you—time, talents, skills, money. Who will be the first person or organization you will help?

It all starts now.

NOTES

Havin' Church

"Keep Your Mind on Jesus," copyright Ida Atchison, 1957

"Call Him Up," Ricky Grundy and Herman Netter, copyright 1980, 2012, Savgos Music, Inc. and Grundy Boys Music

The Grand Finale

"His Eye Is on the Sparrow," words by Civilla D. Martin, 1905

Two Hearts, One Beat

"Trust and Obey," words by John H. Sammis, 1887.

Can God Call a Time-Out?

"I'm Just A Nobody," copyright Doug Williams, Melvin Williams, and Leonard Williams, 1985